LOST FATHERS

LOST FATHERS

*How Women Can Heal from
Adolescent Father Loss*

Laraine Herring

■ HAZELDEN®

Hazelden
Center City, Minnesota 55012-0176

1-800-328-0094
1-651-213-4590 (Fax)
www.hazelden.org

Library of Congress Cataloging-in-Publication Data
  Herring, Laraine, 1968–
    Lost fathers : how women can heal from adolescent father loss /
      Laraine Herring.
        p. cm.
    Includes bibliographical references and index.
    ISBN-13: 978-1-59285-155-3 (pbk.)
    ISBN-10: 1-59285-155-X (pbk.)
      1. Young women—Psychology. 2. Adult children—Psychology.
    3. Daughters—Psychology. 4. Fathers and daughters. 5. Fathers—
    Death. 6. Absentee fathers. 7. Loss (Psychology). I. Title.

  HQ1229.H59 2005
  155.9'37'08352—dc22

                                                                    2004059923

09 08 07 06 05   6 5 4 3 2 1

Cover design by Theresa Gedig
Interior design by Ann Sudmeier
Typesetting by Stanton Publication Services, Inc.

In addition to personal experiences shared by the author, other vignettes about
grief are found in this book. These vignettes were created by the author to represent common experiences of women who are healing from grief. Any resemblance
to a specific person, living or dead, or specific events is coincidental.

All poetry throughout the book, except for the poem by Ikkyū on the dedication
page, was written by the author.

Ikkyū, "Ten dumb years . . . ," translated by Stephen Berg, from *Crow with No
Mouth*. Copyright © 1989, 2000 by Stephen Berg. Reprinted with the permission
of Copper Canyon Press, P.O. Box 271, Port Townsend, WA 98368-0271.

for dad

jai bhagwan

"Things hidden come rapping at the door."

UKRAINIAN PROVERB

Ten dumb years I wanted things to be different furious proud I
still feel it
One summer midnight in my little boat on Lake Biwa
caaaawwweeeee
Father when I was a boy you left us now I forgive you

—IKKYŪ, FIFTEENTH-CENTURY ZEN MASTER

Contents

Acknowledgments

SO MANY PEOPLE, personally and professionally, have worked in my life to bring this book to life.

I thank my co-researchers for their honesty and willingness to share their stories; Sister Teresa McIntier, for her compassion and guidance; Dr. Cappi Lang Comba; Dr. Tim Ayers; Leslie Simon; Hope Edelman; Antioch University Los Angeles MFA Program; the Barr-Harris Children's Grief Center; Prescott College; Sally Lara and the Phoenix branch of the National Council on Alcoholism and Drug Dependence; New Song Center for Grieving Children; Camp Paz; and Catholic Social Services for insights and a chance to grow, fail, and try again. I honor the women of Prescott, Arizona, for holding my heart; the faculty and students of the Phoenix College Creative Writing Program for allowing me to share their stories; and Yoga Pura for giving me breath. I thank my agent, Linda Roghaar, for her belief in this project; my editor, Becky Post, for her wisdom and guidance; and Dalena Watson, who showed me I had more depth inside than I ever thought possible.

The scholars, thinkers, and teachers Carl Jung, Joseph Campbell,

Clarissa Pinkola Estes, Carol Pearson, Maureen Murdock, Rollo May, John Bowlby, Therese Rando, J. William Worden, Elisabeth Kübler-Ross, Marian Woodman, Linda Leonard, Mihaly Csikszentmihalyi, Viktor Frankl, James Hillman, Kenneth Doka, Natalie Goldberg, David Whyte, and Amrit Desai: I, and this work, are richer because of you.

The poets Ikkyu, Rumi, and Hafiz: you are the Heart unfettered.

Carol Anne Perini taught me that I could love and be loved without conditions; Alma Luz Villanueva believed in my talent; Gayle Brandeis cheered me on; Trina Belanger helped me live the writer's life; Jeffrey Hartgraves gave me titles; and Mary Sojourner gave me passion. Arvin Loudermilk and Mike Iverson held me in the dark; Robin Craig gave me bear-energy; Carolina Morton showed me grace; Anastazia Millison put red in my life; Barbara Joy gave me trust; Ruth Davis restored my faith; and Gus Brett broke me open and stayed to help me pick up the pieces.

For my family: my mom, sister, and stepfather, thank you for my stories. Thank you for my foundation and my life.

Namasté.

Ghost Dance

Trapped

It is only a few moments
on the clock of my life.
Each year that passes increases the space
between when we were family
and when you were dead.
The who I was when we were family
stopped moving somewhere on the way out of the coffin
toward the sunflower field.

It is very gray here
because even though the clock stops
time still passes
and gray looks like blue or yellow or green
whether my eyes are open or closed.
It's the same.

Let me sleep here wrapped in the gauze of my wounds.

When the coffin is closed
and gray turns inside out I will scarcely notice
the colors that dance on the black canvas spinning away.

I will have died with you,
your skeleton locked around me.
If only you would move your arm I could stretch,
but you can't because you're dead
and I, dutiful daughter,
will never break that bone.

I sleep in the arms of a ghost. You'd be surprised how strong those arms are. How tightly they hold. How much they resist release. I pray to an absence—a hole that has been with me so long it fills my spaces. I seek counsel and direction from the silence, and in my search for connection no one can penetrate the cavern.

I have constructed this ghost, cell by cell, since I was a child. My sanctuary is in the invisible. After suffering for twelve years with degenerative heart disease, my father died when I was nineteen years old. He had a massive heart attack the summer of my seventh year. My childhood was wrapped around his dying and his death, and my adulthood has been wrapped around an attempt to make meaning of these events and to undo some of the beliefs that developed during the time of his dying.

When I first thought about writing a book about adolescent father loss and its effects on women, I thought I'd see what other information was out there. I found wonderful books on mothers and daughters. I found books on fathers and daughters when the father was abusive, drunk, or absent. I found books on fathers and sons and the importance of that bond. I couldn't find a book, in the mainstream press or in academia, that specifically addressed the intimacy issues of adult women who experienced the death of their father while in adolescence. Was the taboo gender relationship that develops when a daughter hits puberty still too unsettling to discuss? Was it because women, in relationship to men, were still not considered important enough to write about? Or, worst of all, was I the only one who had experienced this type of loss, so was there no need for this discussion?

Once I began the research for the project, I discovered that this loss is a hidden loss, a disenfranchised grief. Adolescents, ages twelve through twenty-one, are often overlooked in the grieving process. They look like adults, so they are not always given the tools necessary to work through the grief that occurs in their particular developmental phase. As I started my investigation, I discovered many women willing to share their stories with me, and many women grateful to talk about something that in many cases no one had ever asked them about. Through their stories, I gained connection and the confidence to pursue this project.

Addressing this topic through a feminist lens, I have struggled to locate my identity separate from the male—separate from the father, lover, friend. As I became an adult, I saw men differently. I saw that none of them was my father, yet, paradoxically, all of them were. All of them were, in some way, leaving me.

For years, I thought my inability to connect with men stemmed from the betrayal I felt from my father's death. I have come to see that even though that single event brought its own set of difficulties, the roots of my intimacy problems began long before the day of his death, September 18, 1987. They began when, as a child, I learned of death and illness. I learned that what was strong yesterday could be struck down today. I learned of impermanence at a time when I desperately needed to believe in the idea of safety and security—no matter how unrealistic that concept was. The coping skills I developed during childhood turned into belief systems that prevented me from living fully in adulthood.

For twelve years, while growing up, I saw my father every day for the last time. I wondered if he would be alive when I came home from school, or if he would have fallen asleep in the orange La-Z-Boy chair, tired from a trip to the grocery store, or if he would be dead in the bedroom, mouth open to the sky. I'd walk past his sleeping body and listen for the breath, the rasping in and out of a life. As each day passed and he left us a little more, I pulled back, re-created and re-imagined him as a new form. A form I could control. A form without ending. During a series of surgeries, I saw the man I loved the most leaving cell by cell. The man I would create in my mind would stay. This man would hold me and whisper stories in my ear and show me, for sure, which path to take, which man to love, which doors to open. As the man in front of me grew weaker, the ghost became stronger, and on the day my father died, the ghost took over as everything my father could never be—physically strong, a protector, a warrior. Permanent. I held hands with this ghost and promised an eternity to it, even as its fingers robbed my flesh of warmth.

A dance with intimacy is precarious at best. Everyone comes with baggage. Everyone comes with expectations. Everyone hopes the other person will somehow keep the cold away, keep the wind from breaking down the door. When one sleeps with ghosts, the ghosts have their objectives as well, and one of their biggest objectives is to stay alive. When the time comes to kill a ghost you've created, you'll be surprised at the army that is there. Ghosts come in many sizes and shapes. Some are silent. Some talk nonstop. But all ghosts need a host body to live off. Parasites, they rely on the living for fuel and energy. When too much time passes, the host and parasite change places, the host sustaining its life from the dead.

Adolescence is our most traumatic passage since birth. We are shaking off the familiar. Rejecting home. Experimenting with ways of being in the world. When death pulls us, attaches us to that which we should rightfully be leaving, what do we do? At fifteen, sixteen, nineteen, twenty we don't have the tools or life experiences to adequately and gracefully move away from childhood into adulthood while at the same time maintaining a healthy relationship with the dying parent. Most of us can't even ask for the keys to the car without a traumatic event. It is the exceptional child who understands unfinished business, who understands that we have this moment—no more, no less—to be authentic in our relationships. Paradoxically, although children tend to live almost religiously moment by moment, it takes the wisdom of years to understand the fragility and the impermanence of a single moment. When death comes to an adolescent girl's home, I contend she will do one of two things (and most likely parts of both) in an attempt to reconcile her own changing body and world and the newness and vastness of her future with the heaviness and permanence of death inside her home. She will either run as fast and as far as possible away from the dying man, or she will attach to him, and subsequently to the family, for far longer than is healthy.

I did both. I moved out of the house at eighteen but couldn't make the move to another city where I had been offered a scholarship to college. In truth, I remember very little of what actually happened during the last years of my father's life. I remember clearly what went on in my mind and the fantasies I constructed around his dying. And it is that reality that I operated by through adolescence and into adulthood.

This story begins in 1976 and is still ongoing. I have traveled through depressions, addictions, abusive relationships, and self-imposed solitude. I have moved from Christianity to atheism to Buddhism. I have moved, at last, away from my family and into my life as mine, not in the shadow of one who is dead. For fifteen years after my father's death, I defined myself by his loss. Through this book, I hope to share with you that struggle and offer you ways of working through your own intimacy issues and moving through loss and transition with as much ease as is possible for you.

I am not finished with this process. I know these issues will surface periodically throughout my time on this planet. What has shifted in me is awareness, and compassion for self and others, and a conceptualization of my role in the permanent impermanence of our existence. I am not offering quick fixes. I am offering a process. When a young woman loses the most significant man in her life while she is growing up, she fears that loss again. Many behavior patterns surface, which will be discussed throughout this book.

There are many paths on the attempt to reconnect with the missing man. Only through acceptance of this primal, first painful separation can we see the beauty of the cycles of life each of us must go through. We can no more avoid or change these cycles than we can stop our monthly blood flow or the shifting of our bodies as we age. I hope, through sharing my own experiences and struggles, I can help you connect to this unnamed loss and help you create a future in which, though you are shaped by your loss, you are not defined by it.

CHAPTER ONE

Grief Counseling

I BELIEVE THAT WE ARE STORYTELLING CREATURES. Our stories are influenced by many factors. Our family of origin, our socio-economic status, our race and gender, and our religious and spiritual beliefs all contribute to our individual story, or, as Joseph Campbell called it, our "personal myth." This book will address these themes specifically as they relate to adolescent women and adult women who have experienced the death of or abandonment by their father figure. We will explore through stories, case studies, expressive arts concepts, and meditations, how these issues may affect future intimate relationships.

We create the themes and threads of our stories. Indeed, we are creating them all the time. This creation process is often so instinctual that we are not aware of what we are forming, and how this story can affect our lives. Only when a storyline is challenged do we realize how strongly we have held on to the plotline and how resistant we are to any revision, even if the current story is not working.

We can get stuck in this personal mythology when we continue to use outdated belief systems. In other words, sometimes our stories stop serving us and begin to actually hinder our ability to live fully in the present.

J. William Worden, an internationally acclaimed grief counselor, developed four "tasks" that a griever must go through to complete the task of mourning. They are:

Task 1: to accept the reality of the loss

Task 2: to work through to the pain of grief

Task 3: to adjust to an environment in which the deceased is missing

Task 4: to emotionally relocate the deceased and move on with life[1]

Therese Rando offers a six-step process for grief work. Her six steps are:

1. recognize the loss
2. react to the separation
3. recollect and re-experience the deceased and the relationship
4. relinquish old attachments
5. readjust to move adaptively into the new world without forgetting the old
6. reinvest[2]

It is easy to see the similarities between these two paths through grief work. When thinking about our lives in terms of a story, I offer these four steps:

1. Remember what your story is.
2. Reconnect to your story and honor how it has served you.
3. Release your story if you choose, or recommit to it if you feel it is still working for you.
4. Re-story your life in a way that is now in alignment with who you are and where you want to be.

Each person's grief process is unique. Offering a variety of paths to do the work helps provide a place of power for the griever. This book will focus on a story-based process of grief.

RECOGNITION + ACTION = WHOLENESS

Recognition of our problems plus action steps can equal wholeness. We have the power within us to make our lives what we want them to be. We set our limitations and we set our goals. We have the ability to rewrite these limitations and goals at any time. But we cannot shift the storyline of a reality of which we are not conscious. This book will help you find out what unconscious patterns may be governing your life.

Life is always changing. John James and Russell Friedman, in *The Grief Recovery Handbook,* define grief as "the normal and natural reaction that occurs whenever there is a loss of any kind."[3] This loss could be a move, a divorce, a loss of a pet, or a job change, in addition to a death. Since change is an inevitable part of living, the grieving process should be a natural and intimate part of our lives. Unfortunately, this is rarely the case.

Grief is not spoken about in our culture. We hide our grief behind addictive behaviors such as workaholism, alcoholism, compulsive spending or exercise, and over- or under-eating. If we want to manage our addictive behaviors we must come face to face with why they are there in the first place. This often means facing our shadow side. Some people assume the unconscious is the shadow side of the personality. This is partly true, but as Jungian analyst Marie Louise von Franz wrote in her 1964 essay "The Process of Individuation," "the Shadow is not the whole of the unconscious personality. It represents unknown and little known attributes and qualities of the ego—attributes that mostly belong to the personal sphere and that could just as well be conscious." She goes on to say that "the Shadow becomes hostile only when s/he is ignored or misunderstood."[4]

There is a Ukrainian proverb that states, "Things hidden come rapping at the door." Like the Big Bad Wolf, they will huff and puff until they blow the house down. In layman's terms, what you refuse to look at in yourself will eventually surface in your life, either as a surprise or a welcome guest. I believe we have the choice to embrace this shadow and work with it, rather than invest in the energy to fight against it or keep it buried. After all, to destroy it is to destroy half of our being.

DENYING THE SHADOW

Society teaches us well to deny the shadow side of ourselves. In pledging allegiance to the light, we disown all parts of the darkness. Our dualistic society bombards us with these messages every day. There is a clear "good" and "bad" or "right" and "wrong." However, a balanced life works like the phases of the moon. There are times when it is all light and times when it is all dark, but fifty percent of the time, it is a mixture of both. For this not to be would be unnatural. Why do we expect more of ourselves? Carl Jung, in *The Archetypes of the Collective Unconscious,* warns us that:

> . . . consciousness succumbs all too easily to unconscious influences, and these are often truer and wiser than our conscious thinking. Also, it frequently happens that unconscious motives overrule our conscious decisions, especially in matters of vital importance.[5]

What does this mean to us? To me, it means that most of us go through our lives in a state of relative lack of awareness. Things are as we perceive them to be, and we allow that to be good enough, without further exploration. We don't have the time or inclination for self-discovery, so we continue to flounder in storylines that do not serve us. We continue to make choices based on reaction rather than conscious choice. We usurp ourselves and remain victims to the unconscious forces at work.

This may still sound confusing. After all, we think we know what we're doing. We think we make the best choices every day. Our self-sabotaging behavior is quite sophisticated. In most cases, it has been developed and honed for most of our lives. To give you a simple example of what I mean, I'd like to tell you a story about my path toward becoming a writer.

My Own Storyline

I remember the day I learned to write. The magic of the graphite mixing with the yellow newsprint paper gave me a thrill I had never experienced. These gray marks made stories! And these stories connected us to each other! I knew this in my body at five years old. I loved the feel of the pencil in my hand and I loved the slate smudge that grew larger on my palm with each line I wrote. Quotation marks gave me a thrill that I could only express by writing line after line of dialogue on the blue-lined writing paper. I could make people talk! It was incredible. I can honestly say I've never experienced anything like it again.

When I was in first grade, I wrote my autobiography. It was almost sixty pages long, complete with illustrations, an acknowledgments page, and a price of $1.95 on the cover. I intended to be the youngest person in the world to publish a book.

Although I had supportive parents, it didn't take long in the outside world to realize that being a writer was not a practical thing to do. Issues about making a living kept surfacing. In school, we read story after story by writers who ended up broke, drunk, or dead. These were our great writers. And they were men.

The women we read were considered odd and reclusive like Virginia Woolf or they committed suicide like Sylvia Plath or they wrote "light" fiction, the grocery store romances. None of that was appealing to me. Still, I kept a journal in my backpack filled with dark and brooding adolescent end-of-the-world poetry that supported my isolationism and reclusive tendencies. I wore a dark blue trench coat and combat boots to high school. I decided I would have to major in English in college because then I could teach. And so, the decision made, the storyline I set in motion proceeded to play itself out.

The storyline, in this case, was *I do not believe I can be a writer. I must construct a different life.* And life worked out exactly as I had believed. I majored in English and entered the work force, though not as a teacher but as a copywriter. I wrote copy for the backs of shampoo bottles and hair spray cans. I wrote brochures that convinced women they would have a whole new lease on life if they bought our new wrinkle cream.

But I still wrote stories and poetry. I dabbled in the occasional creative writing class. Covertly, I sent stories out into the world.

My first story was published in 1992 in a tiny, Xeroxed publication called *The Bohemian Chronicle*. I realized when that acceptance letter came that it only mattered to me, and that this process, this writing life, was indeed solitary, and that if I was going to succeed in it, I would need to embrace that solitude and do the work and release the outcome.

Standing in my one-bedroom apartment with the handwritten letter I had waited my whole life to receive, I knew that this was a turning point. This could either be the beginning of something else, or it would be good enough. This acceptance came with no money, of course. Just a sample copy of the magazine for my portfolio. But it awakened something inside me that I had given up on. However, at this point, I had a good job. I had health insurance and two weeks' vacation. I had my own desk and computer and direct deposit. So I returned to my job and stayed there for eight more years. But that bit of myself that had been awakened would not go back to sleep.

Unconscious Belief Systems

During this time I read a lot of self-help books, trying to connect to the life I knew I was supposed to be living. One of them suggested a belief system exercise. The instructions were to identify a key issue, begin with the sentence "I believe _____ are . . ." and start writing, using your non-dominant hand. That means if you're right handed, write with your left hand, and vice versa.

So I began with "I believe writers are . . ." and began writing. I was shocked. My list included everything from "broke" to "alone and lonely" to "drug addicted." There was not one positive belief in my psyche attached to the writing life. No wonder I couldn't commit to a life change. I not only didn't believe it was possible; I believed the repercussions would be incredibly self-destructive.

If I had been asked directly if I believed any of those things, I would have answered truthfully, "no." I would have certainly said I didn't believe I would be a drug addict or an alcoholic. Yet my unconscious mind believed these things and was therefore acting as an agent on my behalf to prevent me from achieving my goals.

This is a simple example that illustrates the power of the unconscious mind to govern our conscious lives. It was not until I addressed these beliefs and *rewrote them* that I was able to move fully into my truth as a writer and teacher. The key point I'd like to stress is that I was *unaware* of these beliefs. This is a critical concept to understand as we work through the topics in this book related to intimacy and father loss.

NO "GETTING OVER" A LOSS

The grief counseling component is straightforward. Everyone grieves differently, at different times, in different ways, with different intensities. There is no universal storyline for grief. What is universal is that if we love, we experience loss, and if we experience loss, we must grieve. Grief is a storyline for every human on the planet. The variations occur in the ways we deal with that grief.

The cornerstone for effecting positive change through grief counseling is to find a way to re-create a relationship with the deceased that does not hinder our ability to live fully in the present. This is J. William Worden's fourth task: to emotionally relocate the deceased and move on with life. Just because someone dies doesn't mean our relationship with him or her is over. That relationship is transitioning. Certainly, it is not like it used to be. Certainly, there are many things we wish were still the same. But in truth, that relationship has just entered a new phase of development.

I think it's important to address the idea of "getting over" something. There is no "getting over" a loss. There are simply ways of living with that loss. Physically, I moved out of my father's house at eighteen, but symbolically, I did not leave until I was thirty-four years old, fifteen years after his death. I was unwilling to allow that relationship to change due to numerous factors that will be discussed in the following chapters. My relationship with my father has shifted dramatically since then. What was once a barrier, an army of soldiers in front of me, has now become a presence behind me and within me, quietly loving me, yet allowing me to be who I need to be in this life. The ghost of my father, once reinforced steel, is now a soft gauze of energy, shaping to my form, yielding to my directions.

In my experience, many people find themselves "stuck" in this fourth task. This is the re-storying stage. This is where we have to be honest with ourselves, release what we have been pulling with us, and re-create our lives. This power is within each of us. This work is courageous and often frightening. If you are working with a therapist, make sure he or she is aware that you will be taking this journey. If you are working alone, I encourage you to find a close friend or partner you can utilize while on this path.

HOW TO USE THIS BOOK

Throughout this book, I will refer to the idea of a personal storyline. What am I talking about? Like any good novel, our lives have all the components of a story. We have conflict and resolution, characters, dialogue, and tension. Our days are filled with separate scenes. Some of them are action-packed, while others simply fade into the swamp of memory.

Joseph Campbell's book *The Hero with a Thousand Faces* helps us begin to understand the idea of our lives as stories. Stories have heroes in them. We, as the starring characters in our lives, should be the heroes of our own lives. If we aren't, we might need to look at the storyline we've been living.[6]

What does it mean to be a hero? Aren't heroes perfect? Aren't they brave and courageous? Always male? Not at all. One of my favorite things about heroes is that they fail, often many times, before their final success. Heroes persevere. Heroes grow with each encounter with adversity. They do not have adversity-free lives. In fact, it is the adversity they experience that shapes their heroic path. A heroic life is not a life without tragedy, mistakes, sorrow, and loss. A life is heroic because of those very elements, and because of how a person works with those elements to write a life.

Ideally, we all live our own stories to the fullest degree of authenticity. But all of us, at any given time in our lives, lose sight of our needs and put the needs of others first. Being a hero of your own life does not mean you become a selfish, uncaring woman. Quite the contrary. Just as flight attendants tell us on the airplane to secure our own oxygen mask before assisting others, we must care for ourselves first so that we have something to give to the world.

THE STORY OF YOUR LIFE

Many adolescent women "lose their voice." This voice is what gives us the ability to ask for and receive what we need. When we give the control of our lives over to someone else, complications occur. This happens in intimate partnerships, parenting roles, work situations, and family dynamics. As adolescents, we can observe kids going along with using alcohol or other drugs because someone they wanted to impress was doing those things. We see people willingly get into a car with a drunk driver rather than assert themselves. In more subtle ways, we see women giving up their dreams to follow their husbands to a new job. We see women caretaking to an unhealthy level with their children, spouses, or aging parents. Giving up our voices can take years and it can be almost unnoticeable until the day we wake up and wonder where we went. Sometimes this awareness takes decades.

I believe thinking of your life as a story will help you address the unresolved grief issues you are still carrying. When we think of ourselves as characters, it helps give us a distance from the events and gives us much-needed perspective. If we can look back on our lives in the framework of a novel, we can begin to see connections and patterns we might otherwise be unable to see. We begin to see how we have been served by relationships (other characters) and events, and where conflicts and complications occurred.

When we are unstable, as we naturally are after a death or loss, we are more prone to allowing others unhealthy control over our lives. For example, after my father died, I entered a relationship with a man who, when I met him before Dad's death, repelled me.

After Dad died, the same qualities that repelled me became attractive. The end result was an abusive relationship that continued to affect my life many years after I was able to leave the relationship. I surrendered my Self to this man, and this choice not only complicated my life, but complicated my grieving process as well.

How we create our lives is the key to what we get out of them. No one knows what the next life is about. Use this one fully to discover, uncover, and recover. Some of you may find that you are still in some ways an adolescent, although you may be fifty years old. This is not a failure on your part. Take the awareness you will gain as you move through the book to complete the passage.

WHAT WE BLOCK OUT

Unresolved grief is composed of unfinished business, and that unfinished business may well be related to complications in the natural progression from adolescence to adulthood. Sometimes we block out things. Events may be too painful to process at the time they occurred. This is a body's normal defense to trauma. Remember the body is concerned first and foremost with its survival. It wants you to live. Congratulate yourself on staying alive. However, when we repress memories and experiences, they often have a funny way of emerging in our lives as relationships, addictions, and other seemingly unrelated problems. You've all heard the term *emotional baggage*. We've all got it. It's our unresolved issues. It is important to note that we will have triggers and issues that we will work with all of our lives.

Grief work is not so much about "getting over" as it is about *integrating*—bringing together all the parts of our experiences so we can find a wholeness. This wholeness comes from internal work, not from external consumption. Buying more, eating more, working more, smoking more will not bring you into this space. Internal work requires us to sit still, meditate, and go inward to hear what is underneath the noise and chatter of your mind. This is where the work begins, and it can be frightening. Internal work is warrior work.

Throughout this book I will share examples from my own life

and writings, as well as stories compiled from interviews with other women that I conducted between 2001 and 2003. I have created composite, representational stories for these women. I felt that would best suit the intention of this project. I am not presenting quantitative studies in grief work. I am offering the gift of stories: mine and yours to help us heal.

You may wish to start a special journal for this process. You may wish to contact a friend, counselor, or clergy member. When a person is grieving, there is a tendency to isolate. Take care of yourself. Eat good, healthy foods. Drink plenty of water. Walk or do some other form of exercise. Approach this work, and yourself, with compassion.

Remember, everyone grieves differently. Everyone's path is different. There is no right way to work through this book and no wrong way. My story is simply one woman's story. I hope you can find something in it to which you can connect. I hope that through my sharing, you find the strength to share your story in whatever way feels right to you. I encourage you to work with a therapist if you are able. We all need a guide at some point in our life's journey.

TELL THE TRUTH

My final piece of advice: tell the truth. Many of us have lied to ourselves and others for so long we don't know what the truth is. Be gentle with yourself. Realize that you have done the best you can with the tools you have. Don't judge your past. Learn from it. Grow from it. Make it new. But tell the truth, as you know it. There can be no healing except from a place of total honesty. Love yourself enough to give yourself that gift.

A writing teacher of mine, Peter Levitt, told me to always write on the dying breath. The word *inspiration* comes from the Latin words *in* and *spiro*, meaning *to breathe in*. The word *expire* comes from the Latin words *ex* and *spiro*, meaning *to breathe out* or *away from*. In English, to expire is to die. I offer instead the definition of release. We cannot write, create, or live fully if we are holding on. We breathe in, we hold, we release. It is in the releasing that all change occurs.

Write on the dying breath. We must release before we can re-story. We must release before we can live.

HOW TO WRITE YOUR STORYLINE

There are a few key elements to strong, effective writing:

- risk
- truth
- specific language
- sensory language
- imagery
- revision

Writing is basically just making pictures from words, which combines the two halves of the brain. The right brain (emotional) operates on images. The left brain (logical) operates on language to interpret the imagery. Always begin with imagery and then try to make the translation to language . . . remembering that language is inadequate for what we have to express . . . yet it is the most concise tool we have.

Risk: Dare to do the work.

Truth: Tell the truth, as you know it.

Specific Language: Use details to describe things. Use the right word, not the almost-right word.

Sensory Language: Use the five senses to describe things.

Imagery: Make a picture. Show a scene. Be visual.

Revision: Have the courage to look at yourself with new eyes.

Try to avoid abstract words when you can. If you write "I am angry" ask yourself what you mean by "angry." Try to describe it or give an example. The more specific you can be, the more beneficial the exercises will be for you.

The first time you do an exercise, just let whatever comes out come out. Don't let your left-brain censor kick in and criticize the writing. This is not a book about the craft of writing. This is a book about awareness and healing.

If you look back on your work, you might want to revise. This is not the revision work you may remember from your term papers in high school. You're not trying to make your work suitable for publication. You're trying to better understand you. Revision is a new way of looking at what you put on the page. When we revise our writing, we are actually re-visioning it, that is, looking at it again from the beginning. We are trying to uncover what we really meant to say underneath all those adverbs and adjectives. We are seeking the truth in twenty-six letters. We're going deeper into ourselves by using these keys: risk, truth, specific language, sensory language, imagery, and revision.

We're waking up.

CHAPTER TWO

What Is Adolescence?

THE SUMMER I TURNED TWELVE, my family moved from Charlotte, North Carolina, to Phoenix, Arizona. We moved because the doctors said a dry climate would be better for my dad's health. Though no one spoke of it, it was evident we were moving for Dad to die. He believed three women—my mother, my younger sister, and I—would fare better alone in the West than alone in the South. He was probably right.

At the time, all I understood was that I was being uprooted from everything familiar and thrown into an environment where only creatures with spines and stingers seemed to survive. Our backyard in North Carolina had trees and grass. Our backyard in Phoenix was dirt with a gray cement-block fence. We moved in July. As hot and humid as the South is, no one is adequately prepared for summer in Phoenix. The air is so hot and dry it steals your breath and robs the moisture from your nose and eyes.

When we moved, we left my best friend to face her junior high experience alone too. We left my cat, Charley, with friends. And we came to a landscape where nothing was familiar. Day after day of endless unyielding sun. My dad was actively dying during my adolescence. At the time, of course, I didn't give much thought to what it meant to be an adolescent and what it meant to be in a developmental stage where the goal is healthy separation from the parents, yet be living with a dying man.

How could I separate when any moment we might find him dead? I did not separate in a healthy way. And I had no idea that I didn't. Much of Joseph Campbell's work deals with the importance of rituals to mark our life's passages and the complications that ensue when we are not allowed or not able to mark those passages. In other words, we have to bring one storyline to an end before we can move into the next one. If we have not done that, our stories, *our lives*, can become needlessly complicated, marked with unconscious behaviors and patterns that are attempting to get our attention, attempting to show us what is still incomplete.

We often don't hear these messages; consequently, they get louder and louder, often manifesting in the form of addictions and other unhealthy behaviors. Our bodies hold a great deal of wisdom. Just as our back may hurt if we lift a box that is too heavy, our inner voice of wisdom also sends out warning signs: slow down, change directions, back up.

A MISUNDERSTOOD STAGE

Adolescence is a misunderstood stage. There is a common misconception that adolescence takes place roughly during a person's high school years. This is not accurate. Adolescence is as particular to the individual as the grieving process is. It is connected to the individual's character and personality makeup, not her chronological age. For the purpose of this book, I focused adolescence between twelve and twenty-one years of age. However, many studies stretch adolescence as high as twenty-five or twenty-six. It is worth noting that I don't feel I personally completed the adolescent passage until I was thirty-four.

So what is adolescence? In addition to being a physical developmental stage, is also a psychological developmental stage. To say it is the passage between childhood and adulthood seems too vague, though that's how it's often referred to in society's discourse. We are allowed to drive a car at sixteen. We are given the massive responsibility of controlling several tons of metal at high speeds. We are allowed to vote, join the military, and, for all society's concerns, considered an adult at eighteen.

Are we all "adults" at eighteen? Just because our bodies are grown, have our psyches caught up? When my friends and I were eighteen, most of us thought we were adults. Two decades later, I find very few of my contemporaries who are sure they are adults even now. Our rites of passage are getting a driver's license and graduating from high school. These are focused on outside achievement rather than recognition of the maturity of a person's psyche.

SO WHO AM I?

Just because we are physically capable of driving a car or having sex or renting our own apartment doesn't mean we are emotionally or spiritually ready to do these things. Many of us at eighteen were either cast off into the world or we cast ourselves off into the world to figure out a way to make a life. That existential question that we grapple with much of our lives—*Who am I?*—is the crucial identity question of the adolescent passage.

The now-cliché image of a youth with a backpack on a train heading out into the world to "find herself" is an attempt to figure out the answer to that question. But if we don't know or at least begin the work to understand the answer to this question, how can we hope to make choices in our lives that are healthy and serve our highest good?

One of the characteristics of adolescence is that we come to identify and create who we are based on others. We exist or do not exist based on who sees us. This is manifested in the extreme lengths adolescents will go to to belong to the right clique, to date the right person, to wear the right clothes. Being ostracized from our peers during this passage is one of the worst things that can happen. We need a group to begin to cultivate our own answer to the question "Who am I?" We try things out. I am this because I am not that. It takes time. The stakes are high.

Ideally, when we can begin to have a sense of self without the need for others' approval or recognition, we move toward adulthood. A life with healthy relationships, healthy boundaries, and a strong sense of what is okay for you, no matter what anyone else says, are marks of a mature individual with a healthy ego development. It is this awareness of a sense of Self that I feel best characterizes the completion of the adolescent passage.

This is a defining moment in a girl/woman's life. To simplify, it is the moment when we stop pretending we like Chinese food just because the whole group is eating Chinese food. When we realize that we can eat the metaphoric food that best suits us *without* losing our community or group, we are well on our way.

ADOLESCENCE: A TRAINING PROCESS

I don't believe adolescence is simply a bridge between the two worlds of adulthood and childhood. It is a time of life in its own right. The whole concept of adolescence has evolved as humans have evolved. When life spans extended to only thirty-five or forty, childhood ended at eleven or twelve, around the time of menstruation. Because of the work requirements of pre-industrialized America, children took on roles as adults and parents far earlier than we would find acceptable by today's standards. We now need a longer training period, both intellectually and socially, to function in a technology-based society.

Western society has changed far faster than our psyches have been able to adapt. The changes in the way our culture operates in just the past twenty years have been astonishing. It's no wonder there is confusion around this phase of our lives. Adolescents are their own tribe, and their passage is its own experience, just like motherhood, pregnancy, and dying. Each experience has its own codes, values, and rituals.

Adolescence itself has been disenfranchised. Adults often wash their hands of behaviors they don't understand. At the writing of this book, it is tattooing and body piercing. But not so long ago it was the music of Elvis, and not so long before that it was girls wearing pants. Every generation pushes its boundaries. Adults may perceive adolescents' actions as extreme, but they are simply trying to be seen, acting out the most common of all adolescent behaviors: *see me.* They are trying to determine, "Who am I if I am not seen?" If the adult responds by turning away, the adolescent responds with more extreme behavior.

The adolescent passage for girls is particularly critical. With our burgeoning sexuality and increase in hormonal drive, girls are often the victims of incest and sexual abuse.[1] For many of us, even if we were not sexually abused, we may have given our bodies to another too early, before we knew what we were giving away. We may have experienced jeers and catcalls if our chests were too big or if we still looked "like a boy." Girls frequently lose their sense of self during adolescence.[2]

WHEN GIRLS SILENCE THEMSELVES

I have witnessed how girls silence themselves in my work in the Phoenix area school systems. Girls in the fourth and fifth grade are often enthusiastic and exuberant, interested in being called on and wanting to be seen. But by the seventh and eighth grade, these girls have changed. They no longer want attention drawn to themselves. They are embarrassed when called on, and tend to defer their opinions to those of the boys. This silencing (often self-imposed) of girls' voices during adolescence can have a profound impact on their adult choices.

Rather than risk conflict by stating their own opinions, girls silence themselves. Girls are not encouraged to express their anger. So what does the adolescent girl who desires to fit in and make connections do with her feelings? Often the safest choice to maintain acceptance is silence. If girls do not have access to their own voices, then how can they hope to answer the question "Who am I?"

Researchers Carol Gilligan and Lyn Mikel Brown summarize the problems central to the psychology of women as a desire for authentic connection, experiencing disconnection, feeling unheard and unable to state or believe in their own experiences, and a difficulty speaking.[3] When I was in my first graduate program, I attended a seminar that explored ancient women's texts. We made a cuneiform tablet from modeling clay and inscribed words with a reed, similar to how ancient women would have written. I inscribed the words "Speak the truth" with no real awareness of the impact I would feel by seeing those words every day. Slowly, I became aware of how little I did speak the truth—the *real* truth of my soul—and how often I still, in my thirties, kept my truth silent to preserve the status quo and avoid conflict.

A few years later, in my second graduate program, I met an artist who became a great friend to me. She had made a series of masks that were on display at the college. One of them, hanging in the center of a brilliant red frame, had the caption "Ask for what you need." I was so floored by that statement I talked her into selling the piece. I needed to live with that phrase. Little by little, that phrase changed my life. I was learning to give voice to my Self again, something I had not done since before my father's illness. Learning to ask for what I need and speak the truth helped move me at last out of the adolescent passage into adulthood.

Not only knowing *inside* the answer to the question "Who am I?" but also being able to articulate it to others and the world at large is essential to the completion of the adolescent passage. If adolescence is characterized by changing bodies, a search for both individuality and connection, an answer to the primary question "Who am I?", and a searching for values and ethics that fit who we are, then we can see the complications that can occur in our storyline at this juncture when we are forced to deal with death or abandonment.

When we are a child/adult, we live in a fragile, volatile, and vulnerable place. Issues of separation, loss, and abandonment occur naturally as the adolescent begins to break away from her parents.

If we examine the life of an individual in terms of Joseph Campbell's hero's journey concept, adolescence is the moment of the "call." It is the time when we begin to examine the world around us. We look at events outside ourselves and try to find a place for us in what we see. We paradoxically search for belonging at the same time we yearn to detach. Add the awakening of hormones to the equation, and adolescence is indeed one of life's most treacherous passages.

THE TREACHEROUS PASSAGE

I believe one reason that adolescence is a treacherous passage is because adolescence is the first journey we are consciously aware of taking. Much of our earlier path has been instinctual (learning to eat, drink without the breast, walk, talk, and fight). These things just seemed to "happen" without much conscious thought. Adolescence, on the other hand, although also largely due to instinct and genetic programming, is the first time we are consciously aware of our bodies and minds changing.

The passage through adolescence is also frightening because we do not know that we can survive it. We do not know that there is another side of the shore, and that one day when we enter the next phase of development, we will be able to look back and see adolescence as a guidepost for the next journey. We have crossed over once—we will cross over again. But we can't know that as we shout at our mothers, drive our cars too fast, test the limits of our alcohol tolerance, or stay too long with a member of the opposite sex in the backseat of a borrowed Buick.

The struggle to find the balance is the stuff of life. This is all new territory to the adolescent. She doesn't know what the outcome can be. Part of the danger she is in has to do with her inability to see the large picture. Decisions are made based on limited information because the adolescent has limited experience. Erik Erikson says that the primary psychological aspect of the adolescent is the identity crisis.[4] This is the time when we grow our hair long or cut it short.

This is the time when we *have* to have a particular brand of shoe to fit in or pierce our tongue to demonstrate our difference.

Minimizing the depth of the identity crisis of adolescence does a great disservice to the adolescent and hinders her psychological development. As adults, we may know the truth of the adage "This too shall pass," but the adolescent does not, and to offer up that bit of wisdom as balm for a broken heart or lost class election is to insult the purity and the depth of the journey she is on.

WHEN TRUST FAILS US

The adolescent must learn to trust herself and the world around her. If this trust is not established early, the adolescent cannot develop the faith necessary for a healthy life.

I believe part of the fracturing of our youth today stems from an unsuccessful search on their part for anything in which to have faith. Often, their families let them down. Their governments, their schools, and their churches all let them down.

If they have studied much, they know their very planet may be about to let them down due to overpopulation, pollution, and the destruction of natural resources. Where do they look for confidence? Where do they look for the belief that if they do manage to figure out who they are, there will be someplace, some community, that will accept them? If they can't find that, what incentive do they have to make a difference for themselves or others?

One of the complexities of adolescence is the adolescent's awareness of urges and actions that appear to occur due to no conscious thought or intention. This is frightening at best, incapacitating at worst. During adolescence, the ego is forming. An "I" is emerging; a consciousness is developing. But at the same time, an unconscious is emerging. Carl Jung says, "I use the term 'individuation' to denote the process by which a person becomes a psychological 'in-dividual.' That is, a separate indivisible unity, or whole."[5] Part of becoming whole is recognizing that there is an unconscious part of us that is most often governing many of our thoughts and actions.

Every girl needs a ferryman to help her cross the river. When the mythic ferryman figure in her life is missing due to death or other loss, the journey is complicated. Charles Corr tells us, "Perhaps there are only two things that can really be said to be common to adolescents who are coping with death. First, they are all human beings. Second, adolescents are generally those human beings for whom the developmental tasks involved in establishing a relatively stable sense of personal identity are of particular importance."[6]

BREAKING AWAY

In an effort to create a stable identity for oneself, the adolescent goes through the process of individuation, by which she needs to transform the parental bond relationship. Due to limited skills, most of these transformations are a series of "breaks" until the adolescent reaches maturity and then *returns* to the parent as an adult.

In late adolescence (eighteen to twenty-two years of age), the tasks faced are "forming autonomous lives, developing a clear sense of direction, and entering into lasting, intimate relation-ships."[7] No matter what is going on in the adolescent's life at that time, these transitions still must occur.

When a parent dies, the individuation process is thwarted. The power to break away naturally has been taken from her, leaving one more thing out of her control. As she seeks self-created stabil-ity, she also loses the anchor she has always had in the parent fig-ure. When this loss was not initiated by the adolescent, but by an outside, often unseen force, such as disease or murder, the adoles-cent does not know where to turn for safety. She wants to, and needs to, test the boundaries of her experience, but she also needs to know that there is a harbor to return to. The loss of a parent removes the harbor, leaving the adolescent floating in new, turbu-lent water.

Also, when a parent dies, the trust bond is broken between par-ent and child. The parent is *supposed* to be there when needed. The parent is *supposed* to live until the child is self-sufficient. When this doesn't happen, the adolescent is left with the belief, *supported by experience,* that even the most stable relationships can result in abandonment. This can create a deep-seated fear and mistrust of all relationships, and cause her to shut down emotionally, often for many years.

Even as I become more aware of my feelings of abandonment, I still experience them with each relationship shift. I think one of my core beliefs is an inability to understand *why* anyone would deliberately try to change anything. Since things change all the time, the conflict inherent in this belief system is obvious. To me, people who initiate change somehow become the aggressors. They have taken an action that disrupts my stability and therefore become threatening. I overreact as if I was defending my life, and on a deep level, I am.

Grief is a life process. And, yes, it is one we all go through if we draw breath. But for those who lived with grief from early childhood, their world is invariably colored by those experiences. Their development into adulthood had additional challenges. Just as we all do not develop the same way like cookie-cutter humans, we all do not grieve or react to early loss in the same way. Some translate early loss into risk-taking behaviors, some withdraw from the world, some overachieve, and some are able to open their hearts and welcome love again.

The adolescent passage ends when we are able to stand as whole beings, confident in our choices and direction. This could happen at eighteen. For most of us, it comes much later. It's not about a number; it's about your psychological and spiritual development. Time does not heal all wounds. Time simply passes. We are the sum total of all we have been, seen, and done. Embrace yourself fully. This book is an exploration of our attempts to make a context, to make meaning, not only for the dead bones of our fathers, but for the still moving bones of our own fragile skeletons.

For the exercises in this chapter, let's focus on simply remembering what you can from your adolescence.

Writing Your Storyline

1. Begin to jot down memories and reminiscences about your adolescence. They can be from before and after your loss. Anything or any part of a memory is important. Don't worry if you can't remember everything or if you're not going in chronological order. It doesn't matter. What matters is that you are remembering. Don't worry about whether something is "true" or not. If it is a memory (a storyline) that you are living with, then it is true for you. Truth is fluid. We have to first remember what we think we remember. This gives us the foundation to begin to look at other storylines. You may do this exercise all at once, over several weeks, or over several months. Honor your process.

2. If you are ready to proceed, take an event you remembered that has particular energy or significance behind it. Try to remember the feelings associated with the events. James Pennebaker tells us that it is important to write about the feelings associated with an event, not simply the event itself.[8] See what you can remember. Take your time. Be honest.

3. Write a letter to your adolescent self, honoring who she was and still is, how she served you, and how you honor her. Whatever feelings come up are okay. You may find yourself crying. You may feel apathetic. It's okay. This begins the process of self-forgiveness.

CHAPTER THREE

The Father/Daughter Relationship

IT IS A CRUEL MYTH IN OUR SOCIETY that children don't need fathers. It is even crueler that it is commonly believed that boys need their fathers more than girls do. It is not a more-than-or-less-than scenario. Boys need men in their lives. So do girls. The absent male has become a sad cliché in contemporary times. Some of us never knew our fathers at all. Some of us knew them for a short time before they started a new family with a new woman and children. Some of us had fathers who were physically present but emotionally absent due to alcoholism or drug addiction. Some fathers were emotionally unavailable. Some were incarcerated. Some were abusive—emotionally, verbally, physically, or sexually. Some abandoned us to work. Some abandoned us to death.

More than one out of three children in the United States are living without their biological fathers. This rate has more than doubled since the 1960s.[1]

This chapter will examine what is significant about the father/daughter relationship. How does a healthy father/daughter relationship affect a young girl's development, and, subsequently, what is missing if that relationship does not unfold in a healthy and complete way?

One of the primary tasks of adolescence is separation. How can we separate from a man who is not there, has not been there, or is dying? A part often overlooked in a person's development (story creation) is the idea of the "return." In terms of stories, this is when the main character (you) returns home with whatever gifts and tools you have learned through your separation and immersion in the outside world.

For example, when Dorothy returns to Kansas from Oz, she is changed. It is important for her to complete the cycle of growth by returning home and sharing what she has learned. Without the return, her journey is incomplete. When a girl is trying to complete her normal developmental task of separation and she is unable to finish the journey with a return, complications ensue. In the case of the developing adolescent girl, the return phase occurs when she is able to return to her father (and mother) as an adult, thus signaling the shift in the relationship dynamic from parent/child to two adults.

I remember distinctly the moment everything changed for me. Dad had grilled our dinner that night—steak for him and Mom, hamburgers for me and my sister. *Chico and the Man* was on TV. We had chocolate cake for dessert. Dad sat in the orange La-Z-Boy, scratching his polio-eaten foot with a golf putter. I fell asleep to the ebb and flow of adult conversation. The next morning, our neighbor was in the kitchen. Mom and Dad were gone. Soon, Dad's sister arrived and took my sister and me with her to her home, four hours away. We spent the next several weeks with my aunt, unsure of what had happened.

The next time I saw my father, he was in the hospital. Children weren't allowed into the critical care ward in the 1970s, so we snuck up the back stairs. The daddy I knew played golf every weekend. He went to work in a big office, laughed a lot, and played games. This man's skin was a different color. He was much thinner. All I could recognize were his eyes. I was afraid of him, but being the dutiful eldest daughter, I didn't want him to feel uncomfortable. I couldn't have known that they went to the trouble to sneak us up the back stairs because they were afraid that he would not come home.

I was not prepared for who I saw in the hospital bed. I don't remember if anyone talked to us before the visit about what to expect. I don't know if we would have been able to understand what we would be seeing anyway. Children have no frame of reference for aging and death.

UNTANGLING MY STORYLINE

I remember going home after that hospital visit and being acutely aware that my father was leaving me and that I was powerless to stop it. This flew in the face of a seven-year-old's normal belief of being in the center of the universe. A common belief system of children five to eight years old is that they, through their thoughts or actions, are somehow responsible for the events around them. I was suddenly faced with the realization that I had no power whatsoever to stop this separation from occurring. Furthermore, a new thought entered my mind: *If my father could die, then I could die too.*

I began to construct a storyline of "preparation" for Dad's death, and I began to realize that he was separating from me. Unconsciously, I began to create a storyline of *not* separating from him. It took me until I was thirty-four to see how tangled in this belief system I had become. This is an example of a story I wrote when I was in my mid-twenties and just beginning to become aware of the powerful hold this storyline had on me.

> When I was nine I would lie in bed and plan the details of my father's funeral. I would stay up late into the night, holding my black-and-yellow stuffed tiger, pulling the quilt over my head so I could see nothing and smell only myself and the freshly washed Holly Hobbie bedsheets. I would imagine the whole funeral service. I seated everyone alphabetically. I saw how strong I would be. I would hold my mother's hand and tell her to be strong. I would tell her Daddy was with Jesus now so please don't cry.
>
> I would imagine him dead in a maroon golf sweater, his blue eyes closed and silent. I would visualize his ascension, step by

step, above us in the hospital. I could see his spirit floating in the left corner of the room, a blue throbbing energy cloud, watching the doctors and nurses, straining to stay. I felt him enter my body and tell me he loved me and I felt the jolt in my ribs as he left for heaven.

When I spoke at the funeral I would know just what to say. I meticulously wrote his eulogy and believed that I could touch the mourners deeper with my words for my father than any scripture could. People would hug my mother, in my imagination, and there was plenty of fried chicken and yellow cake and iced tea.

Then it was over and I had been strong for one more night. My pillowcase was cold and wet and I buried my face in it to smell the secure smell of wind- and sun-dried cotton and feel the comfort of my own tears, clammy against my cheeks. I listened for my father's snoring in the next room, and when I heard it, I could rest.

I practiced crying silently for many nights. I could cry until my eyes were mail slots and make no noise. I could blow my nose quickly and efficiently and flush the Kleenex down the toilet so no one would know I had been imagining again. I would bite down hard on my stuffed tiger's tail to control my breathing.

My canopy bed had six white metal bars holding up the pink and white material. Each week I stared at a different bar—memorizing it, accepting it completely into me. I believed that after six weeks of my imaginary funeral I would make all my sadness go away so I could be strong and dependable for Mommy when the time came for Daddy to go.

I thought six weeks was an excessively long time to be sad about anything. I thought I would be ready and Daddy would be so proud of me because I had planned ahead and got my crying over with early. "Very responsible," he would say. "Foresight is very important. Foresight will save you a great deal of pain in this life." Yes, Daddy. See what a good girl I am? I figured out everything. I even made a list of who to call and in what order. I can love Mommy when you can't anymore. I know I can.

I wanted to tell you at breakfast what I was doing. When you were eating your eggs and I was reading the comics, I wanted you to know that last night I made believe that you were dead so I would be prepared. But in the morning you were always so alive I thought I might make you sad if I told you you were going to die. I didn't want you to have to think about it.

When I was nineteen and you did die, I put on mirrored sunglasses and drove the Buick with the radio blaring. I had indeed learned how to cry silently, directing the tears with my eyelashes away from any non-waterproof eyeliner. But I didn't see you in the corner of the room when the doctors and nurses were pounding on your chest and wheeling in plasma machines with blue and green lines. I didn't see you in the corner of the room when I delivered your eulogy or graduated from college or got my first job. I didn't see you in the corner of the church when my mother remarried and my heart split in two.

And I don't see you now, when I lie in bed with my orange cat, Apricot, and slide deep under stiff sheets to insulate myself from the darkness. Sometimes I pull the quilt over my head and inhale my body and press the sun- and wind-dried sheets to my face where tears are hot lava and I wonder, when I was nine, where I thought you'd go, and why I believed I could set the sadness free.

THE "OTHER" IN THE FAMILY

The father/daughter relationship is one of the least researched in our society. Some of this is due to living in a patriarchy, where women's stories are not valued as much as men's, even in this "post-feminist" age. Some of this may be due to the changing notion of fatherhood in America. Women working outside the home are the norm rather than the exception these days. Seeing men in the grocery stores and picking their children up from day care are very recent changes in our society's fabric.

Fathers have traditionally been the "other" in the family—the secondary parent. Dads worked on cars, hid in dens behind newspapers and whiskey, worked twelve hours a day. Daughters have a tendency to view their fathers as heroes, no matter what the father's actual behavior may be.

The father has many tasks in a healthy daughter's development. Fathers help keep the mother/daughter bond from becoming too close. Because mothers and daughters are of the same gender, there can be a tendency for the daughter to over-identify with the mother. Fathers help with this natural separation process. All children are attached first biologically and then emotionally to their mothers. A mother's love is supposed to be absolute (although this certainly isn't always the case). A father's love is not guaranteed.

Through the father, the daughter learns to see herself as a separate person, capable of functioning autonomously in the world. Fathers may dote on their daughters, hold them in their laps, take them to fairs and win stuffed tigers for them. Daughters thrive on this when they are young. Fathers experience the non-sexual adoration of a young girl. This is something fathers will not get from their mothers or lovers.

An eight-year-old girl sees limitless possibility and perfection in her father. Fathers reward this adoration with gifts, special times together, and an awareness that they can "do no wrong." "Daddy's little girl" is a very real component of the father/daughter relationship. Little girls grow with this awareness and believe that this is always how it will be.

However, when girls begin to develop physically, most fathers abruptly pull away, sometimes even harshly. They may pick on their daughter's clothes, tell her to take off her makeup, try to stop her from dating. They often refrain from touching her. What was once a relationship filled with healthy contact dwindles overnight to almost no contact. Fathers are very aware of the incest taboo, and many, in an unconscious attempt to avoid even the slightest hint of inappropriate behavior, pull back entirely from their daughters' lives. This abandons the daughter even if the father is still in the house.

The father may be remembering his own adolescence and sexual activity. He may be having difficulty realizing that his role as the primary male focus of his daughter's life is shifting to the outside world. He may realize that her adoration is shifting to adolescent boys—which he well remembers being.

Even though the adolescent girl's body may look like a woman's, she is still emotionally a girl. The sexual attraction between fathers and daughters is most often unconscious, yet daughters still learn to understand (or not understand) themselves as attractive sexual beings through the relationship with their fathers.

WHAT A FATHER MODELS

Victoria Secunda says, "The greatest impact on a woman's romantic choices and her ability to feel comfortable in her own sexual skin is how her father treated her in childhood."[2] In a healthy family, the father provides the "practice" for a young girl to learn how to interact in the world.

In 1973, E. Mavis Hetherington performed one of the first studies on the effects of father loss on adolescent women. Her findings indicated that the girls of divorced parents behaved in a more flirtatious manner with men. They tended to date earlier and become sexually active earlier. Girls of deceased fathers experienced the greatest discomfort around men. They dated much later in life. They "exhibited severe sexual anxiety, shyness and discomfort around males."[3]

Hetherington's study opened the doors for further research in this area. Prior to her work, the focus had been primarily on fathers and sons and mothers and daughters. Making the connection between a "lost father" and adolescent behavior with men was groundbreaking. Though still under-researched, there is no doubt today that the connection exists.

Young girls often shape their behavior to please their fathers. Secunda's research shows us that the young girl's desire to please her father and the behavior modifications that manifest begin to create what Secunda calls the "false self."[4] The false self is a concept rooted in Buddhism. It is the mask or persona we occupy to meet our needs in any given situation. When adolescent girls begin altering the authenticity of their emotions around their fathers, they are learning how to do that with the future men in their lives.

If Daddy doesn't like loud noises, girls will learn to be quiet. If Daddy encourages debate and discussion, girls will learn to value that. Daughters will go to great lengths to earn praise and recognition from their fathers. If the father is absent, emotionally or physically, girls may try on many different masks and roles to try to win his attention.

Think about this in relation to your own life as a story. Do you find yourself playing many different roles? Do you have the answer to the question "Who am I when no one else is in the room?" It's okay if you don't. Just think about the question. Based on many years of research, I know that I am one of the lucky ones. My father saw me as a person with a mind, opinions, dreams, and goals. He believed in me and trusted me to make good decisions. He didn't treat me as "less than" because I was a girl, and he didn't hold to the traditional gender roles.

I didn't realize until much later in my life how unusual that was. As an adult, I observed that none of my female friends could recall those types of qualities about their own fathers. I had friends whose fathers ignored them, abused them, degraded them, and abandoned them. My father was actively dying almost my entire childhood. Even as he was imparting solid life skills to me, he was still abandoning me to his own death. The storyline I wrote around this experience was that men cared about women. They were sensitive, emotionally available, and interested in women's feelings. But they would leave.

Of course, when I began dating I found very few men who wanted to know me. They wanted to have sex, not conversation. I thought there could be both. When I was thirty-two I met a man who gave me both. He became the trigger for much of my unresolved grief around my dad. This unconscious storyline that I was living out almost destroyed all components of our relationship.

Suffice it to say, my father saw and recognized my heart, and I have been searching all my life for another man who could do the same.

THE FATHER'S DAUGHTER

A common theme for women with lost fathers is the idea of the "father's daughter." Maureen Murdock says, "father's daughters are women who over-identify with, or hero worship, their fathers."[5] These women have chosen to reject the feminine in favor of their father's masculine characteristics. They often have few female friends. By shutting themselves off to half of themselves (their feminine nature), father's daughters feel constantly incomplete.

Father's daughters identify so heavily with their fathers that when they are abandoned for any reason, they may fall into despair, believing they cannot live without this man in their lives. The object of their adoration, their hero-father, is no longer around. Father's daughters have no identity except in the context of their fathers. Where does this leave them when their father is gone?

I don't mean to imply that fathers are all bad or all good. Most men, like most women, do their best with what they have. As we move further into the twenty-first century, male and female roles will continue to blur. Society has changed very quickly. A century ago, most Americans lived on farms or small rural towns. Women did not have the right to vote. Men worked in the fields or in the new factories. Women worked at home. Society has progressed faster than we can adapt.

If a man's own father was distant, abusive, or belittling, most likely he will pass on that behavior unconsciously to his own children. He may view women as "other" and therefore not know how to be appropriately intimate with his own daughter. If he cannot be available to his wife, he will almost certainly not be available to his daughter. As the dialogue opens up about the importance of the father/daughter relationship, I am hopeful this will shift.

Whether your father was nurturing and supportive, caring but distant, absent to work or addictions, emotionally unavailable, or physically unavailable due to death, divorce, or abandonment, where you begin the work is today, with all the elements of the story you have been given. Nothing else matters. You are responsible for managing your own unique life circumstances. The first step, as always, is awareness. Let's begin there. Take out your journal.

Writing Your Storyline

1. What are some positive moments you remember about being with your father?

2. What are some moments when your father let you down?

3. How would you describe your father to a stranger? How would you describe your relationship with him?

4. How did your father respond to your adolescence? Was he accepting? Did he ridicule your changing body? Did he distance himself or become inappropriately close?

5. Finish this sentence: "My father thinks I . . ." Freewrite for fifteen minutes.

6. What smells, colors, and textures remind you of your father? (For example, my father wore Mennen cologne and often wore a green Izod golf shirt.)

7. What did your father teach you about money?

8. If your father were here today, what would you like to say to him? What would you like him to say to you? You might try writing the answers as a letter.

As with all stories, the more concrete our details are, the stronger the story is. Be as specific as you can be. Sometimes one detail can lead you to another.

CHAPTER FOUR

Fathers Who Died:

Long-Term Illness, Accident, Sudden Death, Homicide, and Suicide

IN A GOOD STORY, the plot stays in motion because the main character faces many obstacles that she must deal with. Sometimes she is able to overcome a problem; sometimes the problem is too much for her. Stories and lives keep moving because things change. If nothing changes, nothing happens. Change occurs whether we want it to or not. Sometimes we spend a great deal of energy trying to avoid change or stop it from happening. When I was seven and we learned Dad was dying, I began to prepare early for the ultimate change of his death. I thought if I could work through it *before* it occurred, I wouldn't have to feel it when it did occur. It doesn't work that way.

When does grief work start? We have to return to the moment of change. Depending on your circumstances, the moment of change—the moment when you began to create a different storyline—may have been before your father physically left. It might have been the moment of diagnosis, if your father had a long-term illness such as cancer. It might have been the day he lost his job at the factory because that was the day he began to drink to excess.

If your father was emotionally distant your whole life, the moment of change may have been when you encountered a man who wasn't. That may be what set things in motion for you to begin your exploration into your relationship with your father. Each of us has a different set of circumstances, so each of us has a different starting point.

This chapter will address the many ways we can lose our fathers to death. No one way is better or worse than another. They all result in the absence of a father. Be careful not to compare your loss with someone else's. You are entitled to 100 percent of your grief. You feel your loss 100 percent. Work with your own storylines, remembering that even if you have a twin sister, you both experienced and adjusted to the loss in your own way because you are individuals *and* each of you had a separate, unique relationship to the same man.

THE LANGUAGE OF DEATH

You've experienced the death of your dad and quite possibly the deaths of others. You know that in response to a death people stumble over things to say, if they even bother to say anything at all. You know there is nothing anyone *can* say to make the situation better. You learned quickly that language is inadequate. You learned that even you don't know what to say. Language failed you. Language is a tool to label, explain, express, analyze, and categorize our *experiences.* When we attempt to do these things to *feelings,* we get stuck.

In general, Americans have difficulty talking about death. We remove the sick and dying from mainstream society. We talk of death as if it were an anomaly rather than a natural part of the life process. The medical profession goes to almost obscene lengths to keep people breathing (as opposed to *living*). I think death is viewed as a failure in the United States. This sets people up for complications in their grieving process when death occurs. If dying is somehow a failing, then something could have been done differently to prevent it. Sometimes this is true. Most times it is not.

Children are particularly susceptible to language use when death occurs. Children are literal beings. Metaphors such as "Daddy is sleeping now" do not translate to a child's literal mind. Many children are afraid to go to sleep after being told, "Daddy is sleeping." If a child is told, "Daddy went to be with God," the child may wonder why Daddy chose to leave just then and, in turn, she may be angry with God for taking him away.

Children recognize the severity of the situation. Children realize that their biological survival is linked to their parents. A thirteen-year-old knows she can't go out and work for Microsoft and get her own apartment if her parents die. "Who will take care of me?" and "Where will I go?" are frequent questions in a bereaved child's mind.

Many adults are afraid to talk about death with other adults, much less talk about it with their children. Adults often mistakenly assume that children don't know or can't handle what is happening. They may have a false sense of wanting to protect the child from sorrow. Children are very perceptive. They know things are different. They will have legitimate questions about what happened.

Children deserve the truth. They will process their grief in a healthier manner if they have all the facts. If they don't have the facts, they will create facts to fill in the blanks. They will do what they need to do to make meaning out of chaos. Adults may choose to not expose a child to violent images of her father if he was shot or killed in an accident, but that doesn't mean they can't still use proper terminology and specific language. Adults should always use the word "dead" because children need time to wrap their reality around that word.

I've heard people comment on using the word "dead." "It sounds so harsh," one woman said. It is harsh. It is real. And it is the truth. Without the truth, healing cannot begin. A child should be given as much detail as is age-appropriate. She should be given as much information about the disease or the cause of the accident as possible. Children will keep asking questions. Adults should keep answering to the best of their ability.

Now think about your own situation. What language was used concerning your dad's death? Did you feel you had anyone to talk to about the details? If it was a sudden death, did you understand how it happened? Do you yet?

UNFINISHED BUSINESS

All of us have unfinished business in our lives. Through the course of living a life, we make mistakes. We don't behave perfectly. We hurt others and others hurt us. This is life. One of the key components of unresolved grief is the amount of unfinished business a person has with the deceased. Unfinished business is the stuff that makes our psyches heavy. It's the stuff we carry from one apartment to the next, one relationship to the next, repeating harmful patterns until the day we realize we are heavier than we need to be. Our lives are needlessly complicated by things we are carrying that no longer serve us.

Tim O' Brien's short story "The Things They Carried" (from the book by the same title) tells the story of a platoon of soldiers in Vietnam.[1] The characterization of the men is only through the objects the soldiers chose to carry with them. In addition to describing each object, O'Brien gives us the weight. This reinforces how important the objects were. For anyone who has ever traveled, the suitcase that didn't seem so heavy when you packed it suddenly weighs a thousand pounds by the time it's been up and down stairs and on and off trains.

In terms of grief, John James and Russell Friedman describe unfinished business as wishing things had been "different, better, or more."[2] Most of us have unfinished business in relationships. Even if we are more conscious now and have cleaner relationships, most likely there are quite a few relationships from the past that have some unfinished business attached to them. When we talk about parents—our first and most primary relationship, the relationship around which some of our biggest storylines occur—we are bound to have unfinished business.

We have expectations of whom and what we think our fathers should be. One of those expectations is that your father is present and supportive. If you're reading this book, your father wasn't those things and is dead, wasn't those things and is still living, or was those things and is dead. Any way you look at it, he is unavailable. This can create a snag in the storyline. What do we do when something is not what we expect it to be? Most of us get angry and resentful. Some of us get sad. All of us, as we experience life's inevitable disappointments, must learn to integrate this storyline of loss if we are to find peace in this lifetime.

Phrases like "I wish he were here more often," or "If only my dad had done X," or "I am the way I am because my dad did (or didn't) do X," are storylines setting traps for your own growth and development. Yes, we can certainly acknowledge that things may or may not have happened, and we must acknowledge the feelings that surface as a result of that, but we cannot put our futures and hearts on hold indefinitely.

Unfinished business is connected to expectations. When expectations aren't met and we carry that resentment with us, it morphs into unfinished business. It's easy to say, "The past is the past. Let it lie." But until we understand and integrate the effects of the past on our current reality, we are tied to its control. While it's true we cannot change the past, if we ignore its impact on our current lives, we close our eyes to the fullness of our experiences. We have been shaped by our past. The key for us today is to embrace it, integrate it, and use it to propel us into a future we consciously create, rather than keep us hopelessly tied to longings we can never satisfy.

Remember, to desire is a normal part of the human condition, but when we expect a particular outcome from a desire, we are set up for suffering. Wishing our father was still here is normal. Holding on to the disappointment that will occur when this expectation is not met will make your life heavy. Take care not to shame yourself for any choices you have made. Every step and misstep in your life has brought you to this point today.

Writing Your Storyline

1. Imagine you are carrying a backpack. In this backpack are all the things you carry with you. These could be memories, words, hurt, sorrow, or joy. They could be memories of a time you felt loved or safe. They could be ghosts of people and relationships who are no longer in your life. They could be job responsibilities or family responsibilities. They could be addictions or an illness. Start by making a list. Next to each item, assign a weight. For example: "Memory of being with my ex-lover: 4 pounds." "Guilt because I was out of the country when Dad died: 25 pounds." Don't judge your list. After you finish your list, take a walk, make a cup of herbal tea, or call a friend. Congratulate yourself on making yourself aware of these things.

2. Pick the three items in your backpack that are the heaviest. Write or tell the story of each item. Remember to be as specific as possible. Remember to use concrete details. In addition to specific images, remember to equate your feelings with it. Whatever you feel is perfect. The work is in your heart, not your head. Let the intellect be a tool to provide language for your heart.

   • If you cannot recall or access your feelings, make a note of that. Don't judge it. Just notice it. If you cannot access feelings, you have given yourself a great signal for where you may have blockages. Hearts shut down when they don't feel safe. If you don't know what you feel, that's okay too. Write that down. When we feel safe and secure, we have uninterrupted access to our feelings. When it seems too dangerous to feel because feeling might make us vulnerable or leave us open to an attack or further abandonment, we are denied access to our hearts. Wherever you are is perfect. Practice being here. Now.

3. Now let's focus on your dad. How many of the items in your list were related to your relationship with your father? If any were related to your relationship with your father, choose one or two items and tell the story. Include how it was, how you want it to be, and how you feel about it. Use specific details and images.

LONG-TERM ILLNESS

Cancer, heart disease, Parkinson's disease, and AIDS are just a few illnesses that can affect our fathers and consequently our families. What does it mean to get a terminal diagnosis? After all, each of us will one day die, so what makes a medical diagnosis feel so much different? For one thing, now there is a timeline. The person receiving the diagnosis now has six months, ten years, ten days. Of course, no one knows for sure what the exact timeline will be.

Even as we are suddenly aware of the finality of our father's time on earth, we still do not know *when* that will occur. Doctors are often wrong. This uncertainty is characteristic of children growing up in homes where the father has a long-term illness. Some questions the adolescent may ask herself are:

- Is today the day he dies?
- Will I come home from school and find him dead?
- Will I get what he has?

In homes where there is little communication, the adolescent may not even know what the father has or how the disease is going to progress. Good communication within the family is essential to deal with the long-term illness of the father in a healthy way. Unfortunately, this is rarely the case.

What do you remember about your dad's illness? How did it change the way he looked or behaved? How did those changes affect you? How did your mother respond to your father's illness? What do you remember being told about your father's illness?

When we write stories, we learn that a character who is ill can easily become the most powerful character in a story, even though he or she may have very little physical strength at all. This is because when a family member becomes seriously ill, it affects the whole working dynamic of the family. We will examine family dynamics in greater depth in chapter 7, but for now, it's important to understand that everyone has a role in a family. Sometimes these roles are "assigned," sometimes they are self-imposed, but a family functions or *dys*-functions based on how these roles are carried out. If your father went to work and your mother stayed home with you and your siblings, then when your father became ill, most likely your mother had to leave the house to go to work. If your mother's role suddenly shifted, someone then picked up the duties your mother used to perform. This may or may not have been your situation, but if your dad died from a long-term illness, you can be certain that the illness affected the entire family.

Can you remember what was different in your family after the diagnosis? Did your parents' behaviors change? Did one or both of them become more distant? Did your mother or father begin abusing a substance? Did they become fanatical about a religion? Did one or both of them become more needy? What about you? Did you find yourself staying home more or avoiding the house?

Because America is so uncomfortable with the subject of death, when it shows up in our own house, we often don't have good tools to process the changes. Our friends and co-workers most likely don't have good tools either, so we are subjected to heartless things people say in an attempt to be kind. You may have heard "He's in a better place now," "At least he isn't suffering anymore," or "He had a good life." What kinds of things do you remember being told?

These statements may or may not be true intellectually, but since grief work is done in the heart, not the head, these statements are not helpful when you are on the receiving end. James and Friedman call these types of sayings "grief myths."[3] We don't know what to say, so we say what was said to us, or what seems to make sense at the time. If your father had leukemia and died when he was fifty-three, it doesn't matter to you that he lived longer than someone else's father. What matters to you is that he is dead. When a family finds out one of its members has a terminal illness, the family begins its first grieving process at that moment.

How We Anticipate Loss

Kenneth Doka identified a series of phases that are unique to the process of long-term illness.[4] He calls the first phase the pre-diagnostic phase. This is when the person (the father) begins to suspect something is not right. He may experience unusual mood swings, headaches, or fatigue. This is the phase that prompted your father to go to the doctor in the first place. If you were a child, it is highly likely you didn't even know something was wrong with him.

Doka identifies the second phase as the acute phase. This is the moment of diagnosis, the point of no return. In stories, this is the climax. As news of the diagnosis sinks in, families may experience anticipatory grief. This is partly what it sounds like—a reaction to the loss that is about to occur. But it is also much more than that. Therese Rando delved deeply into the study of anticipatory grief and she offers the following definition:

> Anticipatory grief is the phenomenon encompassing the processes of mourning, coping, interaction, planning, and psychosocial reorganization that are stimulated and begun in part in response to the awareness of the impending death of a loved one and the recognition of associated losses in the past, present, and future. It mandates a delicate balance among the mutually conflicting demands of simultaneously holding onto, letting go of, and drawing closer to the dying loved one.[5]

Families experience anticipatory grief as they worry about the future ramifications of the death as well as the impact of the death itself. It is very important during this phase to maintain as much communication as possible. All too often, this is not done. Family members and the dying person grieve in silence and alone.

Children who are not privy to the facts of their father's illness may create fantasies that are far worse than the actual illness. When we don't have accurate information to deal with a situation, especially as children, we create a series of facts to help us make sense out of it. Great literature and the storylines of our lives come about from an attempt to make meaning from chaos. We will adapt by whatever means are available to us in order to make our current reality make sense. If we don't have all the facts, it is easy to see how we can create unhealthy belief systems and storylines.

The Chronic Phase

Doka's next phase is the chronic phase. This phase can have many additional stressors. This is the phase when "the goal of medical treatment is still to seek a cure or extend life." It is filled with doctor visits, hospital stays, and various pharmacological treatments. It is indefinite, since no one can predict the moment of death. Many friends and extended family members who were there at the diagnosis have gone back to their regular lives.

The plans of your family are now contingent on the progression of the illness. In my situation, I turned down scholarships to three four-year colleges and chose to attend the local community college for my first two years precisely because I was afraid Dad would die when I was too far away to get back. People will often put their plans on hold, which causes stress for both the dying person and the family.

Diseases have patterns. For example, leukemia has a pattern of remission and relapse, while some kinds of cancers have long, slow declines. The patterns of the disease and the uncertainty of those patterns, combined with false hopes of a cure or permanent remission, cause additional stress to the family. This roller coaster of emotions exhausts families.

When a person suffering from a long-term illness dies, the survivors may feel a sense of relief. This is usually followed closely by guilt for feeling the relief. It is normal to feel relieved. You are able to begin again after the death occurs. Your life had been put on hold throughout the course of the illness. In some ways, there can finally be movement. It is natural not only to feel relief, but also some excitement about the future. This in no way diminishes your love for your father and it doesn't mean you're glad he is gone. You had been living in a traumatic situation for months, maybe years. It is over and you can now begin to move into a life where death is not the focus. This is healthy.

The Shadow of Trauma

Some clinicians, Rando included, assert that people who live with a loved one who is dying experience many of the characteristics of post-traumatic stress disorder (PTSD).[6] Trauma has traditionally been defined as an event that is unusual; that is, not part of the course of ordinary life. People get sick and die every day. This is considered part of human life's natural processes.

True trauma, as commonly related to PTSD, is of an extreme nature, such as war, being mugged or raped, watching the bombing of the Twin Towers, or being in an earthquake or flood. It is not my intent to denigrate the depth of the trauma of these types of catastrophic events. I simply want to point out that many of the same symptoms of PTSD may be present in people—especially children or adolescents—who live with a dying person.

Children's awareness of life, death, and personal security have not been fully realized. If a parent is dying and the child is under eighteen, the child may indeed feel that her life is in danger. Questions such as "Who will care for me and feed me?" are real life questions to a child who is unable to go to work and care for herself. The child certainly experiences feelings of helplessness, loss of control, and panic as the death of a parent becomes imminent.

Recovery Phase and Terminal Phase

Doka's final two phases in the process of a life-threatening illness are the recovery phase and the terminal phase. Sometimes patients experience a time when they and their doctors believe they have been cured (the recovery phase). This can create changes within the family and the patient. Many experience an increased love of life, while some may feel trapped in jobs they don't want anymore because of insurance concerns or fear of not being able to find other work.

My dad underwent a series of surgeries in the twelve years of his life after his heart attack. Each surgery brought a renewed sense of hope and health, but each one was ultimately unsuccessful. No one would hire him because of his health risk. He—and, by default, our whole family—had to reevaluate the future. As *his* life became less and less what he had expected, so did our lives.

When the patient enters the terminal phase, doctors are no longer trying to cure or maintain the disease. The focus is on making the patient comfortable. Families may have to decide about terminating treatment or withdrawing life support. The choices made during this phase can have a long-lasting impact on all family members.

"Unacceptable" and "Acceptable" Diseases

The type of illness your dad was diagnosed with was also a contributing factor to you and your family's grieving process. Although there is no "good" chronic or terminal disease to have, the way society views or labels a disease can affect how the family copes. HIV infection and full-blown AIDS are the best contemporary examples of highly stigmatized diseases. In the 1980s, when no one knew how HIV was transmitted, victims were often isolated from normal support systems and medical care. Even though we now know much more about HIV, there is still a social stigma around the disease. We may feel empathy for the young child who contracted HIV from a blood transfusion that we do not feel for a middle-aged man who contracted it from unprotected sex or needle use.

Some of these belief systems are simply the human mind's attempt to create meaning. If we can affix blame for a tragedy on a person's behavior, then that makes more sense than the seeming randomness of some illnesses. We live in a universe governed by cause and effect. However, the causes for much of our lives' traumas are still unknown. An earthquake occurs because it is in the earth's nature to shift, not because a group of people's behavior affected the geological rhythms of the planet. The more we learn of genetics, the more we see that people may be prewired to succumb to certain illnesses. Certainly, behavior and environmental factors can exacerbate a situation, but still "stuff happens."

Think about the type of disease your father had. A person dying from liver cancer who was an alcoholic may be treated very differently from a person dying from liver cancer who did not engage in high-risk behavior. *It is normal to try to find reasons for why things happen.* But remember, even if you can find a reason—such as the chemical company dumped toxic waste into the water supply, which caused the cancer in your father—it doesn't change the fact that someone is dying. Nothing can change that reality.

Smoking contributed to my dad's death. He grew up in the 1940s and 1950s in North Carolina tobacco country. He smoked multiple packs of cigarettes a day from his teenage years until 1976. After his heart attack, he never picked up a cigarette again, but the damage had been done. I know in 1950 no one discussed the health risks of smoking. But I also know Dad made a choice to smoke. There were other factors that led to his death: his personality type (very type A), his family history, and his earlier bout with polio that weakened his entire body. There were causes, and some of them were behavioral, yet that knowledge doesn't change the fact that he is dead.

Dad's smoking manifested in my life, though. I cannot date a man who smokes. I can't stop the projections in my mind of his eventual death. I'm afraid, so I avoid the scenario. Others may stay far away from people who drink, eat meat, or don't exercise. It is difficult, once our lives have been shattered, to enter the world again. It is normal to cultivate behaviors that you feel will keep you from experiencing such loss again.

Knowledge Is Power

I volunteered at Camp Paz, which is a weekend camp for grieving children. Every Saturday night, a medical doctor joined us for a question and answer period. The kids were allowed to ask any question they might have about the illness their loved one died from. The doctor answered in a language the children could understand.

Some of the children were afraid they could catch cancer from sitting on the couch where their loved one died. Some feared catching the fatal blood disease that killed their sister. Knowledge is power, and unfortunately, children and adolescents are often not given straight information about what is happening. The adult might not understand either, especially if lacking in medical training, and many doctors don't take the time to speak with anyone besides the adult.

It is natural to want to understand the disease that killed your dad. It's never too late. There are many reputable medical Web sites available today. Take the time to understand the illness. If you are concerned it could happen to you, see what preventative steps can be taken to possibly avoid that outcome. Begin where you are.

Writing Your Storyline

1. What do you know about your dad's illness? Describe it as fully as you can.

2. What specific changes in your father, physically and emotionally, do you recall after he was diagnosed?

3. What specific changes do you recall in your mother and siblings after the diagnosis?

4. What can you remember about the day you found out about your dad's illness? Be as specific as possible. Recall smells, light, sounds, and colors. Tell the story of that day.

5. How were you told about your dad's illness?

6. What is the last thing you remember saying to your dad? Be honest. Was it as you would like it to be? If not, rewrite it. You

can write a letter to him telling him what you would like to have said.

7. Think of any moments of change that occurred in your family while your dad was dying. It's okay if you don't think they are pertinent. Write them down anyway.

SUDDEN DEATH

Sudden deaths are caused by strokes and heart attacks, accidents, homicides, and suicides. Sudden loss is a death with no prior warning. Families have no chance to make things right, no chance to say they are sorry for the fight over breakfast, no chance to say "I love you." When death occurs suddenly, you may find yourself totally disorganized. Doka gives three broad problems for survivors of sudden loss. They are:

1. intensified grief
2. shattering of a person's natural world
3. an unexpected series of concurrent crises and secondary losses[7]

You will see that many of the characteristics of grieving are similar throughout this chapter. Since every situation is unique, it is impossible to provide absolutes. In accidents, homicides, and suicides, there very likely will be the added stress of police involvement, the media, and/or a court trial. We've all seen the news reports when a small child has drowned in a neighbor's pool and the newscaster, with every bit of plastic sincerity she can muster, points a microphone in the face of the grieving parent and asks, "How do you feel?"

It is one thing to share your grief with close friends. It is quite another to have your grief minimized and publicized on the ten o'clock news. If your dad died suddenly, take a look at all the factors discussed in this chapter. Don't feel that you have to fit in a particular category. Life is not that neat. If something strikes you as authentic to your experience, honor that. This is your journey.

Sudden death creates an unexpected gap in our lives. The

trauma of finding our lives disrupted in such a major way will linger with us forever. The way you were notified of the death was a significant factor in how you proceeded with your grief work. The type of support system available to you after the death is also very important. For the adolescent, this may have been particularly challenging. You may have been (normally so) on the outs with your mother. Your peers may have had little experience dealing with death. You may have found yourself ostracized by your group of friends, or they may have done the best they could, but offered words that inadvertently hurt.

These factors apply to long-term illness as well, but it is worth noting that the nature of a sudden loss is a complicating factor in the grieving process. Sudden death creates a grieving process with a longer shock phase. Remember Worden's first task (from chapter 1): to accept the reality of the loss. For sudden losses, this may take up to a year or more, longer than with other types of losses because there was no preparation or warning.

Heart Attack and Stroke

Though not as dramatic as a violent death, the sudden death of a parent due to heart attack or stroke produces many of the same responses in the survivors that violent deaths do. Heart attacks and strokes are among the leading causes of death in the United States. Often there are no warning signs. You may have left for school and come home to find your father dead. He may have had a heart attack on the train to New Jersey or on the assembly line at work.

No matter the set of circumstances, he was here and then he wasn't. This is a monumental shock. One day you were fighting with him about borrowing the car and the next day his place at the dinner table was empty. Maybe he missed your band concert and you were furious with him, only to find out he had a stroke at work.

Heart attacks and strokes do not allow for final good-byes. You may wonder if he died alone. You may wonder exactly what happened. What did he think about? Was he afraid? Stephen Hersh tells us "survivors of a death of a loved one from heart attack and stroke live with many of the same after effects as survivors of suicide, homicide and automobile and airplane accidents." He goes on to say the survivors of a traumatic death suffer "a uniquely wrenching loss that starts with shock and may end in familial and personal dysfunction."[8]

Accidents

Research on sudden, violent death tells us to expect a four- to seven-year recovery period, acknowledging that recovery is never complete.[9] Vehicle crashes are the number one cause of death in the United States for people between the ages of six and twenty-nine. Every week, 780 people are killed in car crashes.[10] Unlike many diseases, car crashes have a "blame chain." Though very likely there was no *intent to kill* in a car crash, the chain of events can usually be determined: a split-second lapse of attention to change the radio station, talking on a cell phone, thinking about problems at home, anticipating the night ahead, faulty or poorly maintained equipment in the vehicle, poor street lighting, the weather, or perhaps the driver was using alcohol or other drugs.

If a car crash takes a life, it is very likely the crash was violent. The victim's body may be mutilated, burned, or dismembered. People don't often consider the violent aspect of a car crash when dealing with the survivors. Homicides and suicides are clearly violent. Accidents have a different connotation. After all, there was no *intent*. "Vehicular crashes are among the most unanticipated of deaths," according to Janice Lord.[11] People leave for work or for the grocery store and the family expects to see them again soon.

When a family receives the death notification about a car crash, trauma can occur. There is usually an urgent need to go see the body. This can be complicated, depending on the circumstances of the accident. Whenever there is a fatality, law enforcement treats the accident as a crime scene. This will restrict the ability of family members to go to their loved one's body. Sometimes well-meaning people will try to prevent the family from viewing the body because of the body's condition. This is not always a healthy thing. Family members should be prepared for what they will see, but they should not be prevented from seeing it. Viewing the body is a very basic human instinct. It helps us with Worden's first task: to accept the reality of the loss.

The suddenness of a vehicle crash makes this first task so much more difficult. Children rarely receive the death notification first. You were most likely told of your father's death by your mother or another family member. No matter how you were told, the moment you received the news, your life changed forever. You have never forgotten that moment.

The chain of events that occurs immediately after a car crash is crucial to the family's eventual acceptance of the loss. These things—the method of death notification, the viewing of the body, the handling of the event by the police and other professionals—will be lingering in the psyches of the family long after the loved one has died.

There is a traumatic element to all sudden losses. The trauma response affects the survivors before the grief response and must be addressed before the grief work can begin. As we've learned in this book, remembering and reconnecting to the memories of the deceased is a critical part of the grief process. However, with sudden, violent deaths, the memories may be filled with gruesome imagery of what the survivors believe happened to the body. When remembering "is accompanied by traumatic imagery, the value of the remembrance is lost."[12] A trauma specialist can be of great service to the family at this time.

PLAGUED BY QUESTIONS

The hopeless pondering of "What if?" and "If only . . ." plagues survivors of car crashes. People try to make meaning out of a chaotic event. They try to create a story that makes sense. Telling their stories is very useful at this time. When the death is sudden and violent, people need to be allowed to tell their stories about the moment they found out. Many times, when the death is from a long-term illness, the story the survivors tell is the day or moment of the death. When the death was sudden and violent, the moment of notification is, for the family and friends, the moment of death. It is the moment when everything changed forever. This is the moment that must be addressed and dealt with first, before moving to the other tasks.

If your dad was killed in a car crash, chances are it made the news in some way. Because of this, other people knew about your father's death without you telling them. Perhaps the general public knew more about the facts of the accident than you did because you were not given all the information. The news may have shown images of the crash site if it was a particularly serious or unusual accident, or if it occurred during a peak traffic time. As an adolescent trying to fit in with her peers, this unexpected dramatic change in your life made you stand out from your friends.

If your dad was at fault and/or there were other fatalities, your situation is further complicated. Not only is your dad dead, but he may be to blame. And if his actions took the life of someone else, you most likely experienced a wide range of conflicting feelings ranging from rage to sadness, guilt to shame. The time has come for you to tell your story.

Homicide

According to the Bureau of Justice Statistics, the homicide rate in the United States was 5.5 per 100,000 people in 2000.[13] This is a slight decline from a rate of 5.7 in 1999. Males are most often the victims of homicide. In 2000, males were 3.2 times more likely to be murdered than females.[14] In data gathered from 1976 to 2000, 76.4 percent of all homicide victims were male.[15]

As you might expect, the reactions to a death from homicide and suicide are similar to those to sudden violent accidents. Trauma theory is still in its infancy. We learn more every day about how the body and the psyche respond to trauma. I feel one of the first psychological responses to a traumatic death is a desperate, almost frantic attempt by the survivor to find the meaning in the loss. Each of us has to have a "personal mythology," a set of beliefs and assumptions about the world. We survive and adapt within the framework of that structure.

When faced with a sudden violent loss, our assumptions about the world are shattered. We ask the question, "Why?" Even if the victim led a life that was more susceptible to violence, there is still no good answer to that question. The "why" question is the psyche's attempt to make meaning, to construct a new storyline in which a homicide can fit.

There is strong evidence to indicate "that the initial trauma causes a permanent alteration in the co-victim's nervous system."[16] This is very significant when looking at your own responses and storylines. As an adolescent, you are still forming assumptions about the world. When homicide enters your worldview, you may never feel safe again. You may have constructed a storyline that reinforces and repeats a belief that the world is unsafe. You may still be working with this storyline, even if the homicide occurred decades ago.

Homicide survivors must also deal with outside elements such as the media, the medical examiner, the coroner, the police inspector and a trial, which may or may not have the desired outcome. Sometimes the crime remains unsolved, leaving the family with an open-ended grieving process.

Sometimes a family is not even able to begin its grief work until the trial is over. Family members may be preoccupied with ideas of justice or revenge or closure. And while it may be important for family members to see the trial through to the end, what they often don't realize is that when the drama and busy-ness of the trial is over, they are still left without their loved one, and they often realize then that their grief work has not yet begun.

UNBEARABLE EMOTIONS

A person will often feel an almost unbearable loss of control when homicide strikes. An overcrowded judicial system, plea bargaining, and long waits until trial dates can add to the feeling of powerlessness. Anger and murderous thoughts and impulses may be common.

These are *normal responses* to a traumatic event. Researchers say that anger is a normal response to any type of loss. For families of homicide victims, the anger may manifest as elaborate fantasies of destroying the one who murdered a loved one.[17] Again, this is normal. The survivor is trying to regain some sense of control.

Many times, people will not express these thoughts because they seem so terrible. They are afraid they are becoming just like the person who killed their loved one. However, if the thoughts are expressed and normalized, the survivor has an opportunity to move on with the necessary grief work. There is a difference between vocalizing normal revengeful thoughts and actively taking steps to enact them. The anger can begin to lose some of its intensity and power when family members can actually express their feelings and vent.[18]

Anger cannot be denied. It will find a way to resurface in your life. *Don't skip the anger work.* Stuffed anger can eventually explode, sometimes violently. Even mild anger can turn into dangerous, uncontrollable rage.[19] We have a legitimate reason to be angry when a loved one dies or leaves us. Death or abandonment disrupts our lives. Even the most flexible of people do not like change that wasn't of their choice in the first place and over which they have no control.[20]

Anger can be deceptive. It can be displaced from past hurts onto a current situation. Anger can manifest as physical illness, and anger can be very difficult for women because of society's judgments of female anger. Recognizing personal anger requires us to be honest and humble about our feelings; only then can we begin to own our anger and accept it as a normal part of mourning.[21]

I recommend working with a counselor for your anger work. The energy of anger is so powerful that it can be very frightening when it is released. Remember, it takes more energy to repress an emotion than it takes to release it. If you have been housing rage in your body for twenty years, you are using your energy reserves to *keep* that anger repressed. Once you are able to safely release that anger, you have all that energy supply to use for positive things.

Some of the exercises on pages 61 and 62 have to do with anger.

Don't skip them. Again, anger is a normal emotion present at most losses. When the loss is sudden and violent, the anger is very much a part of a person's response. *Don't skip the anger work.*

A NOT-RIGHT WORLD

Another characteristic of co-victims of homicide is an unusual amount of vulnerability.[22] This stems from their shattered belief systems about the safety and "right-ness" of the world. We all remember the feelings of powerlessness we felt on September 11, 2001. We spoke of America's illusion of safety being shattered. Even if we did not know anyone who died in the Twin Towers, we all had to find a way to re-story our belief systems around the safety of our country and our lives. This is what victims of homicide must do. They must find a way to create a new order from the chaos.

If your dad was murdered at home, you may have been, and may still be, afraid to be at home alone. You may refuse to walk alone at night or travel alone. You may find you have restricted your own life as a result of your dad's murder. Increased fear and vulnerability are *normal responses*. They are attempts to answer the question "Why?" Examine who has taken your story from you. Did the murderer claim two victims? You and your father?

A STIGMATIZED DEATH

Homicide is a stigmatized death.[23] There are often unspoken beliefs that the victim "let" it happen. Friends and co-workers may assume that the family could have done something different and prevented the murder. This helps those people maintain their illusion that they are safe and that murder could never happen to them or someone they love. This treatment leaves the family isolated and alone. They are wounded again by the abandonment of friends.

Within the family, the same isolation and distancing may be going on. As each family member deals with his or her own feelings of guilt, anger, and blame, the choice is often to pull away from one another and not give voice to those feelings. However, this is precisely the time communication needs to remain open and honest.

It's easy to see how this fracturing of the family system can adversely affect the children. Parents may avoid discussing the murder with their children.[24] Children learn they aren't supposed to talk about what happened. This sets up a storyline for future dealings with trauma. Researchers have found that children who experience the murder of a family member often do not grieve until years later.[25] Many people attending homicide support groups for the first time are there decades after the murder took place. They have finally realized that they must talk about their stories. They must remember so they can release.

Suicide

There are 3.68 million survivors of a loved one's suicide in the United States today.[26] According to the Centers for Disease Control and Prevention (CDC), suicide took the lives of 29,350 Americans in 2000. In 1999, white males accounted for 72 percent of all suicides.[27] Suicide is another stigmatized death. Until the mid-1970s, there was virtually no empirical data on how suicide survivors cope. According to Judith Stillion, Ph.D., suicide research is divided into three areas: "attitudes toward suicide survivors, reactions of suicide survivors, and postvention approach to suicide survivors."[28]

It is worth discussing the attitudes of the general public toward survivors of suicide. Studies have supported the hypothesis that the community views survivors of suicide in a more negative light than survivors of other types of deaths. In a country where it is very difficult to find good support for any type of loss, compounding that with a death that may elicit judgment from the community makes the search for a good support network challenging. For some people, suicide is a sin against God and they are unable to reconcile their love and sorrow over the death with their religious belief system. Some survivors of suicide are unable to find comfort in their faith community. Imagine how isolating this is for the grievers.

Researchers indicated that the responders in their study believed that a survivor of suicide could have taken steps to prevent the death. The survivors were also viewed as more psychologically troubled than survivors of other losses.[29] Higher levels of guilt, shame, and anger are experienced by survivors of suicide.[30] There is no data to support that suicide survivors actually *could* have done anything to prevent the death of their loved one, yet if the general population believes that to be the case, then the effects of that false storyline adversely affect the griever. This is an example of how we live out our storylines and how that affects everything we do.

How was your father found? Who found him? What did his body look like? In some cases, the children find the body. This will obviously create a trauma response that must be dealt with before the grief work can begin. Survivors of suicide struggle with feelings of abandonment. They may wonder what they did that made the victim complete suicide. This is especially true for children, who believe they have unrealistic powers over life and death. Sometimes the victim leaves a note. Sometimes not. Sometimes what is in the note only complicates matters.

Since suicide is linked to other problems, including depression, people may fear they have a genetic predisposition toward suicide. Survivors will tend to relive the last months with the victim trying to find the signs, searching for ways they might have been able to prevent the suicide. Sometimes signs are easy to spot. Sometimes they are not. But whether the signs were clear or not, it is important to realize that there was nothing you or anyone else could have done to stop your father from taking his own life.

Suicide is the responsibility of the person who chooses to complete it. The father who completes suicide leaves a lifetime of unanswerable questions for his family. As an adolescent daughter, you may have felt many strong and conflicting emotions. You may have created a storyline that reinforces low self-esteem and rejection. After all, if your dad was so unhappy he had to resort to such drastic action, how could you expect anyone else to stick around? Maybe your storyline centered on silence, shame, and secrets. Now is the time for you to begin to examine what you have been carrying around with you. As always, be compassionate, be honest, and be gentle.

Writing Your Storyline

These exercises encompass all forms of sudden, violent death. Feel free to adapt what you need and skip what does not apply to you. Again, if anger is a frightening and unfamiliar emotion to you, I encourage you to find professional support. When anger is finally tapped into, its power can overwhelm you if you are working alone.

GENERAL:

1. How did you find out about your dad's death? Tell the story. Were you present at the time of his death? If so, what is that story?

2. Do you know who found your father's body? Who?

3. Did you have an opportunity to see your father's body? If so, describe that experience. If not, how does it feel not to have seen it?

4. Describe the role of the media in your grieving process.

5. How was your father's death handled by your mother and other family members? Did you have anyone to confide in about your feelings?

6. Did you tell your friends about your dad's death? What were their responses?

7. Did you express anger at any time over your dad's death? How did that manifest? How do you express anger today?

8. Finish this sentence: "If I let myself get angry, I will . . ." Freewrite for fifteen minutes.

9. Finish this sentence: "Anger is . . ." Freewrite for fifteen minutes.

10. Finish this sentence: "Instead of getting angry, women should . . ." Freewrite for fifteen minutes.

11. Finish this sentence: "Anger lives in my body in my . . ." Freewrite for fifteen minutes.

12. There are many ways to relieve anger energy in a healthy way. The energy of anger can be transformed into powerful, positive, creative energy, but it must be accessed and felt first. Here are some ways to release the energy of anger:

   - exercise
   - use "scream" therapy
   - punch a pillow
   - take a pool noodle and hit a wall or fence with it
   - throw mud or clay at a wall
   - use a punching bag
   - go dancing
   - visit a therapist
   - write in a journal
   - make a clay sculpture
   - work in your garden
   - play a drum or other percussion instrument
   - rearrange the furniture
   - walk or run

   Physical activity moves energy. One attack on an unsuspecting bedpillow is not going to move all your anger, but it's a beginning. What would it be like to truly scream? How would that feel? How much does your anger weigh? Try to draw a picture of it. Where is that anger in your body? Draw it. Does your anger have a smell? A name? If it could talk, what would it say? Do a dialogue with it. A great place to begin might be, "Anger, I would like to tell you . . ."

13. Finish this sentence: "If I let my anger go, I'd . . ." Freewrite for fifteen minutes.

ACCIDENT:

1. What was the cause of your dad's accident? Be as specific as you can.

2. Did you see the accident site? If so, describe it.

3. How did your friends react to you after the accident? Be specific.

HOMICIDE:

1. What do you remember of the trial? Was the person caught whom you believe murdered your father?

2. Were you present at the trial? If so, describe that experience.

3. How did your friends react to you after the homicide?

SUICIDE:

1. If your father completed suicide, did he leave a note? If so, do you know what it says? Tell the story of reading or hearing what was in that note.

2. Have any other family members completed suicide?

3. How did your friends react to you after the suicide?

CHAPTER FIVE

Fathers Who Were Absent:

Divorce, Abandonment, Incarceration, and Addiction

IT'S FRIDAY AFTER SCHOOL and you are waiting for your dad to pick you up. It's your weekend with him and he is late. Again. You wonder how long you will wait before you decide to call your mother to pick you up. You know he's not coming. You are wearing the pale green blouse especially for him because he once told you your eyes matched that shirt. He calls the next day. Tells you he is sorry. He got tied up at work. You hear the voice of his new wife in the background talking to his new daughter. You don't care, you say. You'll see him next month. You get off the phone, put on your headphones, and turn up the volume.

Fathers are defined as "absent" when they do not interact with their children; they consequently do not play a significant role in their children's development.[1] I believe the absence of a father plays a significant role in his daughter's development. We are defined not only by what we do, but also by what we do not do. If it matters if a father is present, it certainly matters if he is absent.

DIVORCE AND ABANDONMENT

There are many reasons why a father may be absent in his daughter's life. Since this book focuses on adolescents twelve to twenty-one years old, I make the assumption that you at least knew your father in some capacity during early childhood. Though there are certainly many girls who never met their fathers, they are not the focus of this book.

Divorce is one of the most prevalent reasons a father may not be in his daughter's life. More than 21 million divorces occurred in 2000.[2] When parents divorce, the daughter faces many challenges. The man who has been living with the family every day now lives somewhere else. He will be seeing his daughter less frequently. If his relationship with his ex-wife is estranged, it may be months before he sees his daughter. He may vanish altogether for a while. He may already have a new girlfriend. He may even be living in a different city or state. No matter how amicable the divorce was, the daughter will still be left with having to construct a different relationship with her father.

Researchers have identified some likely behavior traits that can surface within daughters when their fathers are absent due to divorce and abandonment. According to Claudette Grimm-Wassil, daughters of divorce or abandonment often seek much more attention from men and boys their age.[3] These women may also be more critical of their fathers and/or have more aggressive behavior with both men and women. E. Mavis Hetherington was one of the first researchers to study the affects of father loss on adolescent girls. Her findings also support these results. She concluded that daughters of divorce were more sexually active and had lower self-esteem than daughters whose fathers died.[4] Other possible qualities of daughters whose fathers divorced their mothers include:

- intensified separation anxiety
- denial and avoidance of feelings associated with the loss of the father
- identification with the lost object
- "object hunger" for males[5]

The Lost Object

Some of these terms may be unfamiliar to you. For example, what does "identification with the lost object" mean? It means you may feel the need to create and shape your life in ways that make you feel more connected to your dad. The "lost object" is your dad. It sounds impersonal but "object hunger" is what researchers call our natural longing for our object of attachment. In infants, the obvious primary object of attachment is the mother because the infant is almost completely dependent upon her. Throughout our lives, our objects of attachment could be a father, a lover, a best friend, a sibling, or a job. When that "object" vanishes, we are left to pick up the pieces.

It can be confusing when someone who was once a dominant part of your life is no longer there. If that person is still alive, you may begin to wonder what you did wrong to cause that person to withdraw his affection. You may feel you are somehow to blame for the sudden shift in the relationship. The important thing to remember is that in your relationship with your father *you were the child*. Children are powerless. They are counting on the adults in their lives to ensure their safety and survival. *You were the child.*

Your parents' roles are to care for and nurture you. If that did not occur, it is not a failing on your part, but a failing on their part. Now that you are an adult, you have the responsibility to work with what you have and take ownership of your current situation, but you are not responsible for your father's behavior.

Girls who grow up with a concerned male in their lives come to know a feeling of acceptance, and they know that they are loved by at least one man.[6] If they do not know this feeling of acceptance as children, they may be hindered in their ability to trust the love of a man when they become adults. If you believe your behavior caused the abandonment, you may be more likely to believe that through behavior modification you can prevent it from happening again. Promiscuity can be an unconscious attempt to gain the affection and love of the man who could not provide that to you when you were growing up.

Franklin Krohn writes in his article "The Effects Absent Fathers Have on Female Development and College Attendance" that when a girl grows up without a father, her emotional development may be stunted.[7] It is important to know that it is never too late to re-parent that little girl. It is never too late to give her the consistent love she did not receive from her father. An intensified separation anxiety may reveal itself to you in terms of clinging behavior to your husband, partner, or children. It may manifest as irrational fear whenever a loved one is late. If you hear about a traffic accident on the news, you may automatically assume someone you love was involved.

This behavior may push partners away. You may feel a constant state of anxiety. People may tell you that you worry too much, but you don't know what to do about it. Every time you and your partner have a disagreement, are you afraid he's going to leave you? Do you find yourself unwilling to bring up things in your relationships that you think may cause conflict? Conflict can be paralyzing to a woman who was abandoned as a girl.

Writing Your Storyline

1. When did you first think your parents might be getting divorced? Describe the scene.

2. How were you told about your parents' divorce? Was it a surprise to you or had you suspected something? Elaborate.

3. What feelings did you experience when you realized the divorce was final? (It is okay to feel things like relief or happiness too—sometimes the family was so tense that the changes can bring relief.) Don't judge your feelings.

4. What specific things changed in your life after your parents' divorce?

5. Finish this sentence: "After Mom and Dad divorced, Mom . . ." Freewrite for fifteen minutes.

6. Finish this sentence: "After Mom and Dad divorced, Dad . . ." Freewrite for fifteen minutes.

7. Finish this sentence: "After Mom and Dad divorced, I . . ." Freewrite for fifteen minutes.

INCARCERATION

We have seen a proliferation of television programs and films dealing with prison life. Reality television shows like *COPS* enthrall us. If the adage "Art imitates life" is true, this certainly is a supporter of that claim. According to the Child Welfare League of America (CWLA), 1.23 million incarcerated men have 1.38 million minor children. Ninety-four percent of all incarcerated persons are men and over half are between the ages of eighteen and thirty-four.[8] The average male offender receives a sentence of 103 months. The years 1985 to 1995 saw the inmate population more than double: in 1985 there were 744,208 inmates, and in 1995 there were 1,630,940 inmates.[9] In America's attempt to get tough on crime, the lengths of sentences have increased, mandatory sentencing guidelines have been put in place, and laws such as the "three strikes rule" have been filling our prisons.

When a parent goes to prison, it is easy for society and the child welfare system to write off the parent as a bad person. Although it is rare for the father to be the sole custodian when he is sent to prison, it could happen, leaving the children as wards of the state. "However, most incarcerated men are not married to or [do not] have an ongoing relationship with the mothers of their children," according to a report by the CWLA.[10] More information is available on incarcerated mothers and the effects of their incarceration on their children than on incarcerated fathers because mothers are usually the primary caregivers for the child. "Many incarcerated fathers have no contact whatsoever with their children," according to the same CWLA report. This absence can leave a hole in the child's life.

When a father is incarcerated, obviously the family's contact with the father decreases or ceases all together. Financial strain will likely hit the family. The relationship between the mother and father is key toward how the future father/daughter relationship will play out. If the mother still cares for the father, she will be more likely to facilitate and encourage visits to the prison or other communications with the father. If the father and mother are estranged, it is much less likely that the child will have contact with her father at all. According to the CWLA, most incarcerated fathers do not expect to be involved in their children's lives upon their release.

Children of incarcerated parents are at a higher risk of criminal behavior themselves. The CWLA estimates that 10 percent of teenage children of incarcerated parents will be incarcerated as juveniles or adults.[11] This alone is a significant indicator that children are adversely affected by a parent's incarceration.

If your dad is in prison, what are the implications for you as a young girl? Incarceration has a large stigma attached to it. If your classmates knew about it, you very likely suffered taunts and other childhood cruelties. You may have felt ashamed of your dad and not wanted anyone to know he was in jail. If people asked you about him, you might have said he was dead, or that you never knew him, or that he was out of town on business. Or maybe you staunchly defended him.

No matter the reason for the incarceration, you most likely grew up with fear and anxiety around the event. You might have found yourself feeling clingy to your mother or caregiver, or you may have isolated yourself. As with many family crises, the children are often not told the truth about what is going on. This misguided attempt to protect them only adds to the confusion. Children must be told the truth, with age-appropriate discretion.

Sometimes the mother is furious with the father, which affects the communications with the children. Sometimes the mother is in denial over the father's actions and cannot communicate accurately with the children. Like any trauma, every family system has its own way of adapting.

When a member of a family is incarcerated, it affects the entire family. An already shaky family system can be shattered when incarceration occurs. Incarceration occurs more often in families who are already living in poverty.[12] Families living in poverty most likely have fewer chances for educational opportunities. Jobs are fewer and lower paying. The neighborhood may be unsafe, adding additional stress to the children. The effects of incarceration on a family are structural, material, and emotional.[13] This means the family system itself must shift to accommodate the incarceration. The family might experience a change in its financial status and security. Also, the incarceration will bring up a myriad of emotions for the entire family that must be dealt with.

If your dad was or is in prison, you have likely developed a mistrust of men. You may have difficulty forming deep relationships. You may have dropped out of school or engaged in criminal activity yourself. Because of the high likelihood that parental incarceration comes hand in hand with many other social and economic problems, you will likely be unable to separate the storyline of your incarcerated father from all the other factors that occurred in your life. Because we are the sum of all our experiences, we have the tendency to merge things together in our minds, making it difficult to specifically identify one issue as "the one."

Writing Your Storyline

1. Were you present at your dad's arrest? If so, tell that story. If not, how were you told about the arrest?

2. What was your father arrested for? What details do you know about the crime? Do you believe your father is innocent or guilty?

3. Did you attend the trial? What details do you remember about it? If you did not, did you want to? Why or why not?

4. How would you describe your relationship with your dad before the arrest and incarceration? What are some positive components? How involved was your dad with the family before his arrest and incarceration? How did this involvement change?

5. Did you visit your dad in prison? If so, describe that experience. How did you feel? Did you want to visit him or did you resist it? What did you notice was *different* about your dad in prison?

6. What immediate family changes do you remember after your dad's arrest? These could include living arrangements, financial difficulties, or emotional upheavals.

7. How did your family handle the incarceration? Was it kept a secret? Was it talked about openly?

8. When/If your dad was released, how did he reunite with you? Maybe you have had no contact with him since his arrest. How have you tried to fill that part of your life?

9. Finish this sentence: "I wish my dad were . . ." Freewrite for fifteen minutes.

10. Finish this sentence: "After Dad went to prison, I . . ." Freewrite for fifteen minutes.

EMOTIONAL ABANDONMENT AND ADDICTION

There are other kinds of abandonment that may not be as recognizable to you because your dad did not actually physically disappear. You may feel like you have no right to feel like something is missing if your dad is still living or successful, or if he "did the best he could." Your dad may have come home every night. He may have always paid the bills. But he still may not have been able to give you what you need. I believe most of us do the best we can with the tools we have to work with. Understanding that intellectually does not diminish the emotional impact of someone else's behavior on us.

We are just recently beginning to realize the importance of the father's role in developing healthy children. But fathers of today may very well have had no role model for involved male parenting, especially with daughters. If they grew up with the belief system that a man provides for his family, he may feel that bringing home a paycheck constitutes fatherhood. His own parents may have modeled that. He may not have known how to be emotionally available to himself or your mother.

Many women lament, "My father came home every night, but I never knew him." This is especially true in families where active addiction was present. Addictions manifest in many different ways, but the effects on the family are undeniable. Addictions keep the addict emotionally unavailable to those close to him or her. Addictions are a mask, a veil that covers the identity of the real person.

All addictions take their ultimate toll on the psyche of the individual addicted. However, many of the most prevalent addictions in America have not only dour personal consequences, but also dour social and family consequences. Alcohol and other drug abuse affects every member of the family.

Addiction expert Claudia Black, Ph.D., defines addiction as the compulsive, continuing use of mood-altering substances or behavior despite negative consequences. All addictions are characterized by denial, preoccupation, loss of control, change in tolerance, and withdrawal.[14]

According to Black, alcohol is the most commonly abused substance along with nicotine and caffeine. Cocaine, heroin, prescription drugs, and marijuana are other commonly abused substances. Behavioral addictions include gambling, compulsive spending, eating disorders, sexual addiction, relationship dependency, and work addiction.

"No matter what the addiction, a person is engaging in a relationship with a behavior or substance in order to produce a desired mood change," explains Black.

Once addiction occurs in a family, it takes center stage to all other dynamics. Black writes, "Loss is integral to addiction; it permeates all relationships. The addict, the spouse, and children of any and all ages experience loss when there is addiction in the family. In the children there is much that doesn't get said that needs to be said in order for them to feel loved. There is much that needs to occur for closeness and intimacy."

On the other hand, many hurtful words and acts do occur in addicted families, leaving all members bereft of dignity and trust. In the past two decades much has been written about roles in alcoholic families. If you were raised in such a family you'll easily identify with the roles:

- the responsible child/the hero
- the acting-out child/the rebel or the scapegoat
- the adjusting child/the invisible child
- the clown/the mischief-maker
- the placator/the caretaker[15]

An important breakthrough in psychotherapy occurred when the client began to be looked at contextually, rather than as a solitary, independent being. Meaning is derived from context. We are products of our past and present relationships. As children, we were shaped by our family of origin, which is our original context. A family is a system, and every family member has a role to play in that system. An addicted family is not a healthy system. It is important to look at the roles each family member played in order to see how your own family dynamic has shaped you.

An addicted family is a family in crisis. It is a shame-bound dynamic. Addicted families keep secrets. Keeping secrets means telling lies. Telling lies about who your dad is creates shame. Internalized shame can lead to emotional detachment and difficulty maintaining healthy intimate relationships.

An addiction does not survive alone in a family system. Each member of the family takes on a role to support the addiction. These may be unconscious decisions. It is important to remember that *as a child* you adapted to a chaotic and dysfunctional situation as best you could. No one in an addicted family is getting his or her needs met. Most often, each person becomes a bit (or more) co-dependent. If your dad was the addict, your mom was addicted to your dad. Her codependency with him allowed the addiction to continue. This does not make your mom or your dad "bad." Your family system was sick, and you, *as a child*, were not responsible for it.

Addiction expert Stephanie Brown, Ph.D., succinctly explains that over time addiction becomes the central organizing principle for the whole family, shaping family beliefs and influencing everything. "The family system becomes distorted, restrictive, and unhealthy . . . there is a big secret, a secret that everyone knows."[16]

Brown's research has found that this family environment of chaos, mistrust, and isolation becomes a trauma in its own right. Brown writes, "The individual who lives in this trauma gets lost, submerged in the increasingly distorted and defended swamp of false reality."

Yes, addiction is a disease. But knowing that intellectually does not alter how you *felt* as a girl and teen growing up in the chaos and insanity. It is not about blame. It is about honoring how you, as a young person, felt. Likewise, grief work does not begin in the head with all its grand thoughts, rationalizations, and explanations. Grief work begins and ends with your heart and its feelings. Because we are compassionate people, we want to understand why and how things happened. This is normal. But understanding the why and the how doesn't change the emotional effect of the event on you. Try to keep that in mind.

Your dad may be fifteen years in recovery now and he may have changed his behavior so much that you can hardly believe he is the same man. If that is the case, he may be able to hear you as you return to your little girl and recall her feelings. If your dad is not in recovery, you will most likely not be able to share this journey with him. The work is for *you*—to help you with your healing. It is to help you write your own story.

If you grew up in an addicted home, feelings may be one of the most frightening things to consider. Maybe your thoughts became more important because they could be quantified. Thoughts and ideas are not as scary as feelings. Thoughts can be proven, argued, and explained. Feelings just "are," and there is quite often no rational explanation for them. If you did not learn how to express your feelings honestly, and/or your feelings were not validated and honored as a child, you very likely avoid intimate choices as an adult.

Grief work can be particularly frightening because it only works once you allow the emotions—no matter how irrational they may appear to be—to surface and move through you. I recommend doing this work with a counselor or other support program such as Al-Anon. You will need support for this work.

Writing Your Storyline

Many of these exercises can be applied no matter what form your dad's addiction took. Do as much or as little as you choose. Be honest.

1. Identify your dad's addiction. If it were an animal, a shape, a color, what would it be? What sound would it make? Try to describe it with as much concrete detail as possible.

2. Can you identify ways your mom made room for your dad's addiction? Was your mom addicted as well? To what?

3. How frequently did you see your father? Were these meaningful contacts? How so?

4. Describe in detail a meaningful conversation you have had with your father. If you cannot think of one, now is your chance to write it and experience it. It's okay to make it up.

5. How did your dad's addiction affect other members of your family? Think in terms of behaviors, language, illnesses, and so on.

6. How did you compensate for your father's addiction? What changes did you learn to make in your own life to accommodate it?

CHAPTER SIX

Broken Passage:
Incomplete Adolescence

I REMEMBER A DREAM from early in my life that has continued to recur. I am an old woman with long gray hair standing in a cemetery. Rows and rows of gravestones stretch in front of me. The day is windy and cloudy and my hair blows in my face. The sky is gray. I hold yellow flowers in my hand. In my dream, I say, "This is everyone I have loved. I have outlived them all." And that is the end of the dream.

This is one of my biggest fears: to outlive everyone I care for. Perhaps my biggest fear is that if I do not open my heart, there will never be rows and rows of people whom I could outlive. If I can't let them in during life, I can't let them in during death. A part of me is comforted by the dream. If everyone I love is dead, then I will always know where to find them. They won't move, leave, or change their feelings for me. They will be there, always, in the ground.

This need to know where people are is also a recurring theme for me. I am afraid people will forget about me. I'm afraid that if they have new friends they won't need me. I have even been known to fabricate situations, especially in childhood and adolescence, to manipulate people to show their care for me. I simply don't trust that people care, and I don't trust that that care will continue.

I used to joke that I would let no one new into my life. "If you're already in," I'd say, "you're in for life. If I haven't met you yet, you'll never get the real deal." This made perfectly good sense to me. The risk of losing someone whom I trusted with my vulnerability was too great. I would control life's constant change by avoiding life.

These behaviors represent the adolescent's search for stability, for control, for order. This is still the child wanting to know, with absolute certainty, where to go for love. The quiet of the dead is deafening. Cemeteries don't move. And though they may not be responsive, they never say no. They never say good-bye. They never do anything unpredictable. I have found so much comfort in that over the years.

Until recently, I was not able to say good-bye to anyone. I stayed in an abusive relationship for two years because I was afraid of saying good-bye. I cultivated intimate relationships with men who were unavailable because I knew I was safe. I would never risk enough for it to matter if they left me.

When I was seventeen, I was angry and in constant conflict with both of my parents. My father was dying. No one was talking about it, least of all me. At school, I fabricated many stories about his dying. Every other week there was a new fantasized catastrophe that struck my family. I left for school before 6 A.M. and put on dark makeup to give the impression that I'd been up all night at a hospital.

I even told one girlfriend my dad had had a heart transplant the night before. I didn't even know if they knew how to perform heart transplants. She looked me dead in the eye and said her father had just died the night before and he was a donor. She was sure my dad had gotten her dad's heart. I looked at her beautiful, frightened face and knew she was lying, just as she knew I was lying. We hugged each other underneath the catwalks in our school auditorium and cried. I have often wondered what was really going on at her house that compelled her to make up a story like that. I have often wondered what was really going on in my house.

I was terrified to graduate from high school. I remember the wind on the football field graduation night. I remember everyone else being excited about being through with school, about the upcoming parties, about the upcoming sex. I was not going to any parties. I was not going to be having sex.

I saw high school graduation as the end of everything. My friends, whom I had just become close with, would be scattered. I knew enough to know that no one stays in touch. I had turned down a scholarship to the University of Arizona in favor of the community college, close to home. I was sure the moment our dark blue caps were tossed in the air, all my friends would vanish. My phone would never ring. There would be nothing left to distract me from the dying.

How does a person grow and develop into a functioning adult? What pitfalls stand in the way of one's journey toward psychic wholeness? Does anyone ever achieve "completed" growth, or is the purpose of life about the process—the develop*ing* as opposed to the develop*ment*?

HAVE I UNDERSTOOD MYSELF?

In adolescence, everything is new, intense, and potentially life threatening—if not always physically, certainly psychologically. Erik Erikson begs us to ask the question at the end of our lives: "Now, have I understood myself?"[1] This question is at the heart of adolescent angst.

The adolescent is beginning to think of herself as a Self—as something that could perhaps be explored and understood. The adolescent begins to realize that she is not only an individual, but is also part of a group—a community—a whole. How to assimilate the individual into the group without losing the Self is one of the primary challenges, not just of adolescence, but also of most of adult life. If I have a Self and I don't know who it is, can I lose that

Self to the needs of a group? Yet if I deny the Self's involvement with the group, can I survive alone?

During adolescence, the individual is experiencing the following changes:

- an expansion of libidinal needs
- a widening social radius
- an increase in differentiated capacities
- a developmental crisis evoked by the necessity to manage new encounters
- a new sense of estrangement
- a new psychosocial strength[2]

This is a tall order for any stage of development. Erikson tells us "a civilization can be measured by the meaning which it gives to the full cycle of life." I believe we can take this as a warning for Western civilization. In a ritual-less society in which we value youth over wisdom and beauty over substance, we leave out three-fourths of the human lifespan, focusing all our attentions on the shortest period of our lives, young adulthood. In order to reach Erikson's ultimate credo, "I am what survives of me," we must first believe we *can* survive, and having accomplished that, we must then actually survive.

The ego is the container we have to do our soul's work. According to Carl Jung, ego formation is the primary goal of the individual for the first half of life, whereas the second half of life is dedicated to transcending and surrendering it. "The ego is the seat of the conscious personality, of subjective identity, the sense of 'I.' It is partial, impermanent and changeable, but believes itself to be whole, permanent and absolute. The ego is the conscious part of the total personality, the Self."[3]

The ego moves through psychosocial stages of development. Adolescence is one of those stages. During adolescence the person is focused on identity versus role confusion, sexuality, and healthy independence from the family. An adolescent's developmental tasks include:

- achieving independence from her family, gradually emerging as a separate person with her own goals and values
- becoming responsible for her own needs, feelings, and behaviors
- integrating sexuality into her sense of identity[4]

The adolescent needs to find that delicate balance between being dependent on her parents and being alienated from her parents.[5]

BEYOND ORDINARY

Who am I? Am I like Hitler or Mother Teresa? Am I perhaps the worst outcome of all, ordinary, destined to make no mark on the world? I think it is the fear of being ordinary, the fear that the great destiny promised to us by our parents may have been just an empty promise—just so much air—that causes teens to take such extreme risks with behavior and emotions. They want to prove that they are not ordinary, and that their lives will somehow matter. It is at this juncture that we need the most care from parents and guardians.

If a parent dies or abandons you during this time, a deep-seated fear and mistrust of all relationships can be created and cause you to shut down emotionally, often for many years. Jan Drantell and Leslie Simon write in *A Music I No Longer Heard: The Early Death of a Parent*:

> The child didn't sign up for the good times with the parents, didn't choose the happiness and love, with the knowledge that things change and sorrow may well follow. A child simply can't do that. A child lives in the here and now as if it were forever, and if the trust in the parent is broken by the parent dying, then there's really nothing to do but despair or shut down. The parent is gone. If that can happen, anything can, and it is better, far better, to believe in nothing, to hope for nothing, to bury one's feelings with the dead parent.[6]

Simon and Drantell also write that the primary life task for the child or adolescent who has lost a parent is to learn to open up to the world again. This process can often take years. Even an entire lifetime. Sometimes the fear is simply too strong. If the individual doesn't have a support system to help, she may not be capable of breaking the pattern alone. "For a child or teenager, the death of a parent is not necessarily absorbed into a reality in a day, a week, a year. It takes a long time to realize what hit us," Simon and Drantell write.[7]

Some of the long realization time is due to the adolescent's inability for foresight. She cannot know what significant life passages lie in the future. She cannot know the depths to which she will miss that parent at these moments—a graduation, a wedding, a first job, the birth of a child. Each of these milestones, and many others that are personal and specific to the griever, trigger feelings of loss. To say this is natural and a part of life does not negate the intensity and the reality of the feelings.

Pat, a forty-year-old single woman, says, "Losing a parent at sixteen made me realize at that age that I have no one to count on and so I've never expected anyone to be there. It made me grow up really fast. I learned I have no one to count on but myself." She is relating one effect of the abandonment she felt when her father died. Her ability to trust in others was shattered.

Ellen, a forty-three-year-old woman, has been married for twenty-two years. Although she has been able to maintain a solid relationship with her husband, she addresses this issue as well. "The loss of my father made the need for male attention stronger. I've always felt vulnerable, needing, wanting." She married at age twenty to a man eight years her senior. "At times, he [her husband] seems the most obvious male figure in my life. I also understand him not to be my father, but my husband. Sometimes, there is some confusion and lines blurring."

"I had to learn to protect myself," says Donna, a fifty-year-old single woman. Donna has had a very successful professional career but struggles with intimacy and romantic relationships. Donna identifies independence as a positive result of her early loss. When we are independent, we learn to protect ourselves. It then becomes challenging to enter a partnership. "I have a fear of losing myself," she says. The search for our identity is ongoing. When we have only learned to count on ourselves, the risk of any compromise to that acquired identity is often too great to take.

"Most of my dreams are about loss," says Gloria, a fifty-four-year-old professional woman. "I'm always getting lost or losing my car in some huge parking lot." Dreams of loss and of being left are very common for people who experience death during adolescence.

I have a recurring dream of a train. Our whole family is on the train for a long part of the trip. The train stops in a small town. My mother, my sister, and I get off the train to buy food. My father stays on the train. The three of us are still in the station when the train pulls away. My dad is standing on the deck of the caboose, waving good-bye. This dream always wakes me up with a deep desperation for connection, and an overwhelming feeling of powerlessness. It also leaves me searching for meaning. If we hadn't gotten off the train, we wouldn't have lost him. My mind seeks the logical causal relationship.

This is a pattern of mine in my personal life. If a relationship ends, I try to figure out why and what could have occurred to prevent that change from happening. I try to find ways I could have controlled the ending of that story.

Laura, a fifty-year-old writer and teacher, has this comment about the incompleteness of the adolescent passage. Her father died when she was seventeen. In her forties, Laura began psychotherapy. "I noticed that I felt the therapist was my father, someone who knew me and could teach me the lessons I hadn't finished learning, like holding the world at bay, dealing with insurance companies, and rooting for myself." This is all too common. Who do we call with questions about the mortgage? Who tells us about IRAs or fixing the lawnmower or the importance of cleaning the rain gutters?

Kristen, a married fifty-three-year-old receptionist, also relates to the need to be independent and the paradox of needing independence yet behaving dependently in romantic relationships. Her father died of a heart attack. "I am very afraid of separation and loss. I think about it all the time. I fear being left alone. I constantly fear the loss of a relationship. My dependency drives people away."

We become our own worst enemy when we seek to cling to those we love. It is most often not from a need to control, but from a fear of abandonment. However, our partners and friends don't know that, and we can very quickly create our own isolation chamber, even while we scream to tear it down.

GREEN-EYED MONSTER

Janet is an eighteen-year-old woman. Her father died when she was fifteen, after a long-term illness. Her reactions to the loss and the connection to her intimate relationships surface as jealousy. She says of her current relationship, "I have been really jealous and insecure. I am always afraid my boyfriend will leave me. I'm extremely jealous of any girls that get near him."

Jealousy stems from a need to control. Many of us who have survived the loss of our fathers value our independence. However, we are often controlling and possessive in relationships—the very qualities that will push us away from relationships with others. I do not think this stems from a desire to monitor every aspect of our partner's behavior, but rather from a cellular fear of losing that person. We believe that if we control them, they won't leave. Or if they do, that leaving won't take us by surprise.

I used to be rabidly jealous. I have worked hard on not manifesting that jealousy outwardly. I have always wanted to "destroy" the other women in my male friends' and partners' lives. I sense this may come from having something tangible to see and attack. A thought pattern that surfaces for me is: *If I remove this obstacle, this person won't leave me.* I feel this belief system has been created because I could not strike out at death and illness. I couldn't see it and defend against it.

I made a joke at a gathering of women who were attending an anger workshop. "Not only do I have no anger," I said, "but the anger I have is blatantly misdirected." For me, jealousy does not come from a place of power, but from a place of fear. Grief work can help rewrite these patterns.

The following piece is an essay I wrote after I cleaned out the "junk room" in my house. This room contained my dad's orange La-Z-Boy chair. I had carried it with me from apartment to apartment to house to house since 1987. This was the chair my father watched television in, slept in, and waited for us to come home from school in. When this chair was filled, my father lived.

The Transition

The chair was never very attractive. Even new. Mustard wool with strands of orange thread woven into the fabric covered the frame. It was never very comfortable. Buttons poked your back when you sat in it. But it was my father's chair. It lived in the den of our house from 1978 until he died in 1987. Then it lived in the den of my house. Up until last week. Now it's gone.

I moved the chair out of my dusty junk room. You know the room. It's the place in your house where everything you no longer need but can't bear to part with goes to rest. I moved the chair outside to wait for St. Vincent de Paul, the patron saint of lost furniture. The chair must have shivered in its springs from the sun and fresh air. So many years it had lived in the darkness. Its cotton stuffing had been removed from years of feline attentions, and the recliner often stuck and required a hammer to push the footrest back down.

But it was my father's chair. It was someplace he sat. It was something he touched. As I grow older, there are fewer and fewer people in my life whom he knew. There are fewer and fewer things in my house that he touched. He spent countless hours in that chair watching the PGA on television. The flat voice of the announcer, "Jack Nicklaus for a birdie here on twelve. He's two down behind the leader, Hale Irwin," floated through our house like background music. The names of the golfers I knew, if they even play at all anymore, are on the senior tour or designing golf courses from glass-encrusted homes.

When we lived in North Carolina, we owned a blue Cadillac that had belonged to Arnold Palmer. It had a white leather interior with maroon trim and a big engine—the kind that never lets you down—unlike your own body. My dad had polio as a child and his legs never worked right after that. He wore shoes with lifts so his legs would be even and to relieve pressure from his spine. But he still strained his back often, asking me or my sister to walk with tiny girl feet on his spinal cord while he lay on the green shag carpet, eyes closed. He loved cars and took extra good care of them. "They have to be my legs," he said. "If the car breaks down, I can't walk to get help." To this day, I change the oil in my car regularly. I balance the tires. Tune the engine. My car has never broken down far from help and never when I am alone. I joke that Dad has become my car angel.

But back to the chair. As Dad got sicker and sicker, he spent more time in the chair. He often slept there. I would leave him asleep in the morning when I went to school and find him asleep in the afternoon when I came home. I would wonder if he had moved at all during the day. The chair was next to the side door, with its gray sunscreens that let people inside see out, but no one outside could see in. We used that door to leave the house for school or dates or for long walks around the neighborhood when being a teenager was too much to handle. Since the chair was by the door, Dad heard the engines of the cars that belonged to the fathers of the boys who came to pick up my sister or me. He heard the engine approach long before we got out of the car at midnight to come inside. He'd flash the porch light three times if he thought we were staying in the car with a hormonal boy too long. How I've wished now for someone to flash the light if I was out too long, or out with the wrong person, or just out of my mind.

Dad sat in that chair and told me about college at Chapel Hill. He told me how he and his buddies would stay out at the Student Union and play "Stewball" and "Blowin' in the Wind" on the jukebox over and over while they played pool. It was in that chair that he told me he was dying and that if Mom found someone else to love, he wanted me to know that was okay with him. He knew I was the child with attachments. I was the child with loyalties. When my mother remarried, I thought of that conversation, but it didn't make me feel any better and it didn't stop me from feeling that somehow everything had been betrayed on levels I had yet to understand.

I have carried that chair for fourteen years. Each time I'd see it, I'd see Dad in it. Sometimes he was asleep. Sometimes he had tea in a cobalt blue cup. Sometimes he was reading a golf magazine. But always, he was there. I'd sit in the chair, recline back until I heard the snapping of the gears as the chair ratcheted into place. Dad heard that sound, I'd think. A thousand times Dad must have heard that sound. I could fall asleep in the chair and press my nose into the itchy woolen fabric and convince myself I could smell Mennen and Listerine. The scent of spicy spearmint aftershave was the possibility that he might have just been there—just yesterday—and if I waited long enough he'd come back.

I searched for a hair, embedded in the weave, that could be analyzed to tell me every piece of genetic information that had made him live—to tell me every piece of genetic information that made him die. One hair that would have proven to me that he had lived at all—that I hadn't dreamt it—one long continuous-loop waking dream in which I had a father and a mother and a future that didn't involve death. Although now I know that every future involves death. To believe in a tomorrow means to believe in the ending of today. But this is a paradox I continue to fight.

I have carried that chair for fourteen years. I have nursed it, the fuzzy dust-covered symbol of my wound, showed it as proof that once in my life I knew this man who left—loved this man who left. Proof, perhaps, that there was a time when I could love a man at all.

Sometimes I think I have invented him. Surely, after fourteen years I have invented the idea of what our relationship would have been today. Surely, I have turned him into something he could never be. But the real pain comes from the fact that I don't know that. Maybe he could have been all that and more. I'll never know. And that not knowing has been a seventy-five-pound, woolly, dusty, La-Z-Boy chair on my back. For fourteen years.

When the chair was out of the house, I felt cold wind cut a hole through my breastbone, its edges raw as unheld flesh. The pain was brief. Few tears. Then longer breaths. The space was just—space.

Heart beat. Thump. Thump. Chair outside, not safe from cold or rain. Unprotected. Vulnerable. Dead. Any hairs remaining could blow away. Any DNA evidence tossed to the azalea bushes or the neighbor's swimming pool. Thump. Thump. Breath in. Breath out. Stand on both feet. Earth spinning in a galaxy bigger than the human mind is capable of comprehending. Desperate— so desperate for connection I hold to anything that feels safe. The fibers from a chair. The melted candle from a birthday cake. I hold and the weight breaks me down, bone by bone, until my perception is ground level—eyeball to eyeball with dust.

The chair is gone. My dad is gone. He wasn't here when the chair was here and he isn't here now that the chair is gone. I'm leaving the space for a while. Letting sage blow through. Letting the edges harden a little—enough so another piece of furniture can go there—one that matches maybe—one that doesn't itch or have buttons that poke me in the back. One that is big enough to hold me and big enough to let me go.

Last night I dreamed of leaving. Leaving the desert. Leaving my family. Leaving my home. I cannot recall a dream in which I was the one leaving. I've had countless dreams of being left—of abandonment in train stations, shipping docks, houses, airports, bedrooms—they're almost always the same. I wave good-bye from platforms to people who didn't love me enough to take me with them. People who had destinies with someone else. In someplace else. My role was to hold others, to support them, to help them until they went away. Each time they went away, I bled. But it was familiar. A vampire, the crimson and salt and heat of my blood nourished me.

In my dream, I went around and said good-bye to the people I loved. I said I would miss them. They shed more tears than I. I got in my car and drove down a wide, black, paved street. The street was lined with blossoming cherry trees and the road curved around the path of a creek. Houses set back far from the street and autumn colored leaves filled lawns that did not require irrigation to grow green. I woke up before I saw the end of the road—my house, my street, my city. But I was driving the car, and sunlight slanted through elm trees from a latitude I did not recognize. I traveled light. Four passengers. The wind, the road, the sun, and the future.

Writing Your Storyline

1. How do we re-story a fractured adolescence? Piece by piece. The Sanskrit word *kirtan* is used in Western context to mean a chant. Broken down, *kir* means *parrot* and *tan* means *mind*. The implication here is that the mind is a parrot. It repeats what is put into it. The stories we tell ourselves, whether they are about Aunt Mabel's fruitcake at Christmas dinner or about our deepest fears of loss and abandonment, create our realities.

   • In order to re-story a life we have to re-create it. This work is done first in the mind.

   • Go to a quiet place. Light a candle or burn some incense. You might want to listen to some soothing music. Turn off the phone.

   • Close your eyes and think back to a moment or a day when you were in conflict with your father. Allow yourself to fully imagine the scene. Take care to notice the place you are in and the dialogue you are hearing.

- Write down any key words, phrases, or images you can think of. How did the conflict resolve? Did it? If it did not resolve, write a dialogue or a letter to your father in which you resolve the conflict to your satisfaction.

- Read it out loud. Then return to the quiet place in your mind and visualize the new scene you have written occurring in your life.

2. This exercise has several parts.

- First, write a list as fast as you can of everything you can remember about your dad. You can include everything from hair color to favorite video or DVD to funniest memory. The more specific you can be the better. Do you remember the last words you said to him? Write them down. Did he say anything to you? If he didn't or couldn't, do you wish he had? If yes, what would those words be? Write them down.

- Next, think of a moment in your future when you think you will miss your dad. This might be getting your driver's license, your graduation from high school or college, your wedding, or any number of significant events.

- Write a letter of invitation to your dad to attend this event. Again, the more specific you can be, the better. Fold the letter, put it in an envelope, and put it in a special place. Breathe.

- How would you have liked your separation from your father to occur? Write a short story or draw a picture illustrating what a final good-bye might look like or sound like to you. Try to use as many sensory images as you can (sights, sounds, tastes). The more specific you can be, the more effective the exercise will be.

- What unfinished dialogue still needs to occur between you and your father? Try writing it to him. Ask him to respond.

You can write down the response or simply listen to it in your mind.

- Identify a few key moments during your adolescence when you wished your father had been alive, or if he was alive, when you wished he had been able to participate more fully in your life.

- What would have helped you in the time immediately after your father's death? It could be an object, a teacher, a mentor, or a friend. Draw a picture in which you are with that thing or being. If you like to dance, try choreographing a small routine incorporating the inclusion of that thing or being into your dance of life.

- Can you remember an object that was significant to your dad, or that reminds you of your life with your dad? For me, it was the La-Z-Boy chair. It might be a pipe or a catcher's mitt or a calculator. When you have the object in mind, describe it in detail. Then set your timer for fifteen minutes and freewrite whatever comes to mind.

CHAPTER SEVEN
Family Dynamics

HUMANS ARE SOCIAL ANIMALS. We are born to a family and that family is supposed to provide for our physical, emotional, and spiritual needs. Since every human on earth is growing and learning, no human on earth can provide a perfect, idyllic home environment. The vast majority of us do the absolute best job we can with the tools we have. Children help parents grow as well. The familial relationship is reciprocal.

Earlier in this book, we discussed how a family is a system. Every member of the family performs a function or "role" within that system. Think of a family as the sum of its parts. Each member is unique in his or her own right, but together they form a unit, and as such, each member is dependent on what the other family members do or do not do. You can also think of it as a business. In order for a business to function properly, each employee performs her job to the best of her ability so that the "whole" succeeds. With this analogy in mind, you can understand that some businesses, some systems, succeed better than others. Some families are better equipped to provide a stable environment.

A question often asked is, "Isn't every family dysfunctional?" I think the answer is yes, to a degree, because each of us is carrying unconscious patterns and belief systems that can hamper our awareness in any given moment. Some families experience a greater level of dysfunction than others. This does not mean these families are made up of bad people, or that the children raised in these families will grow up to face lives of prison and drug use. It just means that we all have varying tools for various situations.

Grief, as we've learned in previous chapters, is not a situation many people have tools for. The death or abandonment of a significant part of the family has repercussions for all members of the family system. First, we'll look at what makes a family system, focusing on the dynamic of a family system where one member is an addict. Then we'll look at how that family system can be affected by the death of one of its members.

FAMILY SYSTEMS

None of us came from nothing. As alone as each of us may be existentially, we are still shaped by our environment and its inhabitants. From our first breath, we are absorbing information. Even if we grow up and reject where we come from, we still must acknowledge the original "data input" we received that gave us something to reject. Even if our family of origin is a group home or a foster care family, that environment shapes how we operate in the world, and I feel it creates our primary belief system about ourselves and our world.

Who am I? Where do I come from? What is my place in the world? Many of us spend lifetimes trying to answer those questions. The first answers come from our family of origin. In my experience, most of the work I have done personally and in a counseling setting has focused on uncovering belief systems, identifying them, and then choosing if or how to revise them for change. Sometimes we don't want to let go of a belief system. Sometimes we are afraid to. That's okay. Once the awareness of the belief occurs, then at least you can make conscious choices about what to do with your life. At any given time in my life, I can identify at least two beliefs that I know are preventing me from living fully. In time, I will let them go. I consider it progress that these beliefs change over the years as I shed old beliefs in favor of new challenges.

Where do these belief systems come from? Some of them, I believe, originate in the family of origin. "An individual's behavior is seen not as the linear, causal product of past events or experiences, but as part of a system of transactions between people that codetermine each other in the present. Behavior patterns mutually evolve. A does not cause B's behavior, nor does B cause A's. Rather, they each shape each other's behavior, and therefore their own."[1]

No wonder the individuation process in adolescence is so rocky. Many don't even attempt it. Not only is an individual in adolescence attempting to become her own person, the family unit is, by necessity, having to change to accommodate the changing child. Thus, the experiences and choices of the *one* (the adolescent) affect the experiences and choices of the *whole* (the family).

UNSAFE FAMILY SYSTEMS

Our family of origin gives us our first idea of what home means. And since an infant is interested in survival foremost, and a human being is incredibly adaptable, as infants we will adapt to whatever behavior is necessary to ensure our survival needs are met. In chapter 5, we talked about the tensions found in addicted family systems. We adapt to our environment to stay alive. When we mature, and situations may no longer be so critical, our belief systems haven't been notified of the change of scene yet, and so they still kick in with the same ferocity as when we were threatened as infants.

Survival belief systems are particularly difficult to rewrite because their earliest purposes were so crucial to our existence. All families have certain mechanisms and structures that allow them to function, according to Stephanie Brown. Parenting roles, for example, maintain a family's sense of balance, or what's called homeostasis.[2] If you throw addiction into a family, the balance starts to shift, and the family makes room for the intruder: addiction.

When a family makes room for this intruder, communication shuts down, roles become distorted and the overall environment becomes unsafe for a child. This kind of environment ultimately pushes individuals into what Brown calls a "loss of self" or "false self." She writes that young children are especially susceptible to this for obvious reasons. They submerge their healthy self to prevent further chaos in the family. "Kids, especially young kids, don't have a choice," writes Brown. "The younger they are, the more their normal development will be skewed by the family's turn toward addiction."

If your father was an addict, it is more likely that you developed belief systems that supported addiction in your own life than if your parents were not addicts. An addict creates a life that reflects the way in which she sees her role in the world. This is by no means an absolute certainty, but we tend to manifest what is familiar to us.

A CHALLENGED FAMILY SYSTEM

Certainly, sometimes a parent or other family member deliberately does something to us to cause us harm. More often, parents are doing the best they can with the belief systems they have. It doesn't take long to see how we can perpetuate patterns through generations. Since the family is a separate unit and has its own survival at its core, you can understand how much fear and anxiety can be generated when one individual attempts to shake the family system.

I believe that when an individual challenges her family of origin, she is challenging her survival on a metaphorical if not a literal level. I think many people keep family secrets or participate in family manipulations to continue to uphold the myth of family unity and ensure the individual's survival. It takes courage to risk the survival of the whole for the sake of an individual. If you have struggled to separate from an abusive or addicted family, you very likely faced resistance from that family, especially if you are expected to collude with the idea that "everything is fine here."

When abuse or addiction exists in a family, Brown says family members make a pact with denial. "Denial says 'It isn't so.' That statement becomes the central organizing principle for the whole family and the first sentence in the family's new identity of 'who we are.'"[3] This denial requires family members to layer more and more denial on top of their feelings of fear, anxiety, anger, and sorrow.

Likewise, even in a non-abusive or non-addicted family, when it's time for the adolescent to take that passage out of the nest and into the world, she often encounters great resistance from home. And she learns, as all of us do, that you can't go home again.

FAMILY CHANGES AFTER LOSS

When someone dies, the role of that family member is left vacant. The remaining family members must fill that role in order to preserve the family structure. Think about your own family dynamic. When your father died or no longer participated in the family story, how did the other family members respond behaviorally? Often the easiest changes to see are economic. Most likely, your father had a job, the income from which was key to the current standard of living. Maybe your mother did not work outside of the home and was completely dependent on your father's income for her survival as well as her children's. Her life, whether she was working outside of the home or not, shifted dramatically to try to compensate for the lost income from her husband.

Perhaps your father was the disciplinarian. Perhaps he was the one who fixed the air conditioner when it broke, or crawled under the house to protect the pipes from freezing. There are any number of tasks, *unique to every relationship,* that must be assumed by someone else in the family structure. So in addition to the normal grief response to a death, a family is forced to renegotiate the roles of its remaining members to accommodate the unexpected absence. This places additional strain on a family that is already taxed by the death.

The strength and functionality of a family is challenged to its maximum when a family member dies. Weaknesses in the family tend to be exacerbated. The way the surviving parent deals with the grieving process is key to how the children respond to the loss. When the surviving parent does not have the appropriate tools to work through her grief, the challenge to the family system is even more intense. Because grief is understood in different ways depending on the age of the children in the family, the surviving parent is left with a daunting task of needing to provide for the grieving process of many different individuals in different stages of cognitive and emotional development.

ADULT "LOOK-ALIKES"

The adolescent daughter often has to assume a role in the family that she is not equipped to handle. Adolescents often "look like" adults. They don't need to be taken care of every minute like younger siblings. They may be able to drive and help run errands. They are aware, at this stage of development, that death is final and they are aware of the depth of the relationship loss. This means they understand that their father will not be there when they graduate from high school or get married or get their first apartment.

Adolescents understand that the family unit is going to have to change. But they may not understand how it has to change or how they can help with the changes. Because the mother is now overwhelmed with unexpected responsibilities and emotional pressure, she might rely on her adolescent daughter to handle some things that she previously took care of. These things could include chaperoning younger siblings, shopping for and preparing meals, cleaning the house, or getting an after-school job to help pay the bills. If there are very young siblings, the adolescent may have to be the sole caregiver while her mother works a second job or takes on additional hours at work.

All of this is not to say that the mother needs to handle everything all alone and that the children don't need to contribute and adapt to the changes in the family. What is often overlooked is that adolescents are still children. They are in the process of leaving childhood and moving into adulthood, but they are not there yet. As discussed earlier in the book, part of the developmental tasks of this period is to separate from the family. In order to separate from the family in a healthy way, the adolescent must feel that the family is stable and able to withstand her departure. She also needs to believe that the family will be there should she need assistance in her new adventure.

The death of the father complicates this process. The adolescent becomes torn between feeling like a very young child as she grieves, and acting like an adult as she takes on a job outside the home. She may have to balance school, work, and family responsibilities at sixteen years old. If she was planning on attending college, those plans might be put on hold. Or she may put more pressure on herself to attain higher grades and get involved in more after-school activities so she will have a better chance for a scholarship because she knows that money is tight. Weekends she used to spend with her girlfriends or hanging out with boys are now spent changing diapers or waiting tables. The final phase of her childhood is taken away.

THE BLAME TRAP

If these scenarios are familiar to you, take care to avoid placing blame on anyone or anything. The key at this point is to look at what occurred for you within your own family dynamic, and look at how that has affected you and may still be affecting you. Blaming does not serve your higher good. It keeps you stuck in resentments and keeps you from moving forward into the life you have today. There is nothing that anyone can do to change what happened to your family after your dad's death. Wishing that it had been different will not serve you.

Use your energy to create your present-day life. Keep in mind, too, that it is not your parents' responsibility to be perfect people, meeting your every need, making no mistakes or bad judgments. They were not put on this earth to serve you. We must take responsibility for the direction of our own lives, understanding that perhaps much of what we are dealing with today came from our childhoods.

No one had a perfect childhood. If you are a parent today, you are not providing your children with the perfect environment.

You are doing the best you can. The more self-aware you can become, the more you will be able to help yourself and your own children.

Take a look back at J. William Worden's four tasks of grief, outlined in chapter 1.

Task 1: to accept the reality of the loss
Task 2: to work through to the pain of grief
Task 3: to adjust to an environment in which the deceased
    is missing
Task 4: to emotionally relocate the deceased and move on
    with life[4]

As each individual goes through these tasks, the family unit goes through them as well. The individual members' processes affect the process of the whole family system. Much of the energy of family members is spent in task 3, adjusting to the environment in which the deceased is missing. They are forced into changes that would not have occurred otherwise. They are attempting to "re-story" their lives in a way that makes sense to them.

BLOCKED COMMUNICATION

Research has shown that communication within the family is a key component toward a more successful "re-storying" period after the death occurs. Researchers recognize that the death of a family member puts intense stress on the family, and, in many cases, the family's structure and sense of identity may be quite different after the death.[5] The more accurate and frequent communication can be among family members, the less complicated the transition to the new reality will be.

Unfortunately, with so few people comfortable with the subject of grief and loss, and so few people with effective coping tools, many families disintegrate under the weight of so much disruption. And, since each person grieves in his or her own way, the methods of grieving within a family unit may be in conflict with one another. One person may cry in public a great deal, while another family member may not cry at all in public, while still a third family member may act like nothing happened.

Without open communication about the changes going on in the family, many members of the family, especially the children, may be left feeling confused and isolated. Children most certainly don't have the tools or the maturity to handle such a profound loss. They are learning how to grieve and process loss by watching the adults in their lives.

Researchers have found that a child's level of adjustment after the death of a parent can be directly impacted by how the surviving parent adjusts to the death.[6] The quality of care provided by the bereaved parent during this period and the degree to which the child's basic physical needs and emotional support requirements are met also can affect the bereaved child's adjustment.[7]

After a parent's death, many changes, such as economic changes, a new residence, a different school, or a surviving parent's remarriage, can occur, which can contribute further to the family's disruption generated by a parent's death and may reinforce beliefs that life is unpredictable and out of personal control, beliefs that can exacerbate adjustment difficulties.[8] I feel this belief that life is unpredictable and out of control also manifests in the child's ability to commit to intimate relationships in adulthood. If early in life we learned that someone we love can be taken away from us at a moment's notice, it can be quite challenging to trust completely in future relationships.

WHAT A CHILD NEEDS

The more a child feels safe talking with her parent about the death, the better chance the child has of moving through task 3 and into task 4. Children need to be able to talk freely with the surviving parent about the circumstances around the death, expressing sorrow and asking questions; these types of communication have been found to be protective against depression in adulthood.[9]

I once worked for a nonprofit organization that focused on grieving children. Children who had experienced the death of someone in their family came to our groups with their other family members and each person went to an age-appropriate group to do grief work. This organization felt strongly that every family member must do grief work, not just one member, in order to have the best outcome. One of the activities allowed the children to write anonymous questions that they wanted to ask their surviving parent but were uncomfortable asking. We took these questions to the adult group where the adults then answered the questions. We took the answers back to the children.

It always struck me how much the children were trying to protect the feelings of their surviving parent. They did not want to upset their parent or remind him or her of the loss. Yet the children had so many unanswered questions: questions about the manifestation of the particular illness, questions about the funeral, and questions about whether or not their parents thought about the deceased at all.

It was very apparent that the children needed to see their surviving parent work through his or her grief. They needed to witness the parent's process as part of their own process. If their parent was trying to be "strong" and not show his or her emotions to the children, it often made the children wonder what was wrong with themselves if they still had emotions around the loss, or it made them wonder if their parent had forgotten the other parent entirely. This exercise was frequently a powerful process. Family members were able to communicate with each other in a safe space. The parents were often surprised that their kids picked up on so much.

Children are very aware of their environment. They are watching and absorbing information all the time. It is healthy for them to witness their parents' grief. They are learning the tools they'll carry with them into adulthood to use the next time a loss enters their lives.

Maintaining open and consistent communication, keeping as much of the family life as stable as possible, and allowing the children to remain children are a few of the things families can do to help children with the grieving process. As you look back on your own family dynamic, consider the shift in roles each family member underwent. Consider what behaviors you picked up from that experience that you've carried with you into adulthood. Honor your family and what it provided for you. Honor each member's best efforts and your own. Now is the time to look at the story that has been created, and see if it is one you want to continue living.

Writing Your Storyline

1. Draw a picture of your family of origin. What do you notice about the positions of the characters? The sizes? Where are you in relation to the other family members?

2. What was different after your father died? Be specific. What new jobs did you have to perform? What new behaviors did you notice about you and your other family members? How did your mother's (or caregiver's) role change? What did you have to do to accommodate her changing role?

3. Describe your relationships with people your own age after your father's death. Were you able to find any support with them? If so, how? If not, where did you seek support?

4. Tell a story of a time you remember after your father's death when you had to do something you didn't want to do. Write about the event, but also write about how you felt during and after the event.

5. Can you identify who took over your father's role in the family? If so, who? How did this change manifest? If no one seemed to fill your father's role in the family, what effect(s) did this have on the family system?

6. How would you describe the emotional health of your family after your father's death? Be specific. Use stories that illustrate the adjectives you are using.

7. How would you describe the financial health of your family after your father's death? Be specific. Use stories that illustrate the adjectives you are using.

8. How would you describe the spiritual health of your family after your father's death? Be specific. Use stories that illustrate the adjectives you are using.

9. One of the most difficult things about working with family of origin issues is working with feelings instead of thoughts. Most of us, as adults, are able to understand why changes occurred after our dad's death. Most of us are able to understand that our mother had to go to work to pay the rent. We understand that everyone made changes to accommodate the loss. However, it is important to remember that grief is not about the intellect. It is not about being able to rationalize, explain, or cognitively comprehend the motivations behind certain actions. Grief work is about feelings. It can be very challenging to admit that you feel anger at your mother for leaving the house when you *understand intellectually* that she didn't have any choice. But until you move back into those feelings, knowing that they may be irrational, even cruel, if they are present, they must be acknowledged or they will continue to block your progress. When you can acknowledge it and feel it, you can move it. If you cannot acknowledge it, you cannot move the feeling. It is not necessary for you to tell your family members about these feelings. This work is about you and your personal growth and well-being. Remember that you absorbed these feelings in childhood, so it stands to reason that they may appear childish to you today. That doesn't make them any less real or valuable to you in your grief process. In fact, it may be a clue to you that you've begun to tap into the authentic feelings. I recommend working with a therapist when doing family of origin work. You will likely need

objective support when looking at these conflicting feelings. Try these things:

- Identify key family members (mother, sister, aunt, brother, and so on) and complete the following sentences for each key family member:

  Mom, (Sister, Aunt, Brother,) I am angry because . . .
  Mom, I am sad because . . .
  Mom, I wish these things had been different . . .
  Mom, I wish you'd been able to . . .
  Mom, I wish I'd been able to . . .

- After you complete the sentence, do a fifteen-minute freewrite for each one. Don't judge what comes up. Just allow it to be. Remember to include your feelings along the way—*whatever they may be.*

10. Take some time to think about what you learned as a result of the way your family of origin dealt with the death of one of its members. What specific things worked for you? What specific things did not work for you? How might you incorporate the things you learned the next time you experience a loss? Honor yourself for what you have learned.

11. Empathy means the ability to identify with another person's ideas and feelings. Empathy is a key component to healthy relationships. Children, because of their developmental stage, often have difficulty putting themselves in other's positions. Now you are an adult, and learning to move into another's shoes can help release some blockages and resentments that are no longer serving you. Take as much time as you need with the following series of exercises. You are going to move into the skin of key family members. Take time to center yourself. Breathe. Choose the person you want to work with first. This may be the person you currently have the most difficult relationship with. Or it may be the person you understand the least or is most similar to you. It doesn't matter whom you start

with. You're going to work with every key family member in your system. You're going to write from the point of view (perspective) of this family member. Start with a crisis moment. It could be the moment of your father's death. It could be the moment his illness began to move in. It could be any other crisis moment that you feel is important to this family member. Begin there. Try to imagine, with your whole being, how this crisis affected this family member. Imagine his or her feelings. Try to feel them yourself. When you feel you have integrated, begin to write a monologue from this family member's perspective. If you need a writing prompt to begin, try "I could never tell you . . ." or "Nothing will ever be the same since . . ." or "If only I . . ." But don't feel you need to use one of these prompts. See what your family member has to tell you through the writing. Be open to whatever unfolds for you. Remember, you do not need to discuss or show this to anyone. This is for your healing. Try again, beginning with "I wish . . ." Let yourself discover. Take this process through all the key family members in your system. This may take weeks. Take all the time you need. Take time in between to integrate what you've uncovered or to process it with your therapist. Honor your courage to do this work.

12. Make lists of the qualities you admire and love about each of your family members. Find a special way to let each one know how you feel. You can write a letter, create a piece of art, tell all of them over lunch or dinner, send an e-card—whatever feels authentic for you. Integrate the things you appreciate about those whom you grew up with.

CHAPTER EIGHT

The Mother/Daughter Relationship

16 May, 1998

My mother sits on the yellow sofa
in front of a lit candle.
I, across from her with my drum.
We are singing songs.
My mother is a Christian in her body
but in her soul she flies.

I am showing her ritual.
She knows from church—stand up, sit down
fight fight fight
but this is not our way.
We are singing birthday songs.
We are celebrating friends.

It is her father's birthday.
He has been dead for 20 years.
We sing to him and she is unsure
but then she smiles and sings,

"Kauko," over and over "Kauko,"
his name.

She is surprised the tears come.
I am surprised.
My mother, ever practical, ever calm
grieves internally
and I see the green glow of her heart chakra
split and split and split again.

My mother carries her pains in her body.
Her thin frame, wide smile, young eyes.
She presses sadness into her belly where it
dances madly in the night and robs her
of her dreams
but keeps her safe in layers of thick wool.

This is the first moment I realize her heart
is ripped apart. From father to husband.
She loved.
She buried.
She wrapped up clothes still carrying the scent of
Mennen and emptied her house.

She looked to the future because that is what you do.
When your bones break you find glue.
You work in the garden.
You work on the car.
You pay the bills.
You cry in darkness.

My mother and I carry the same throbbing
light in our skeletons
we view the daylight through the veil of mourning
and guard with spears of vulnerability
that raw place where stoked fires sear
white hot patterns in our cells.

I wrote this poem after taking a trip back to North Carolina with my mother. It was the longest period of time we had spent together since Dad died. I have resisted writing this chapter more than any other in this book. Last night, I had a powerful dream. My sister and I were with my dad. Mom had been gone for several weeks but was supposed to be back in a few days. Dad called us together to read a letter he had received from Mom. In the letter, she tells him she is never coming back. She tells him she has found a new life in another place. She tells him she loves him, but she simply cannot stay.

In the dream, the handwriting on the letter is my mother's. My dad leans forward a bit, into the letter, as he reads it to us. I think of him, left with the pieces of his wife's discontent, trying to find the words to explain to us why she left. I wake up sick to my stomach. My heart is pounding and I feel very unsettled and insecure. I feel abandoned.

In "real" life, my mother did not abandon us, but I have felt many times emotionally abandoned. Why? What to do with these feelings? What are legitimate feelings and what is simply the child throwing a tantrum because her every need was not met? What can I possibly write about the mother/daughter relationship that will not cause pain to my own mother?

So I have been stuck for several weeks around this issue. I do what I always do when I am stuck. I read books. I try to figure out what I am trying to figure out. But it didn't work with this chapter. I don't have a single female friend who is not in conflict with her mother. I have friends who've written novels about their discordant mother/daughter relationship. I have friends who don't speak to their mothers. What is this about? No one sets out to be a "bad mother"—and what constitutes a bad mother in the first place?

To understand the impact of the mother/daughter relationship on ourselves as adults, we must approach this relationship from the spiral nature that it is. Our relationship with our mother is not linear. It is connected to her mother and her mother before that. We see our future selves in our mothers; our mothers see their younger selves in us. I think one of the complicating factors of the mother/daughter relationship is that it is a relationship that is begun based on total dependence of one on the other. The infant is born believing she is the center of the universe. The mother's body responds to the child's needs for food, for touch, for love. The mother keeps the child warm or cool, changes the child's diapers, and provides food and nutrition.

A MOTHER'S FINITE ABILITIES

The mother, however, was not put on this earth to satisfy her child's every need for the rest of her life. The mother cannot provide for every physical, emotional, and spiritual need of her daughter. She cannot anticipate her daughter's every need and she cannot put her own life on hold to accommodate the demands of her daughter. This awareness of a mother's limitations—of a mother's finite abilities—is a moment of initial wounding for the daughter. It is a *necessary* wounding.

It is vital that the daughter learns and accepts her mother's humanity. This is not always an easy proposition. Our mothers represent to us often everything we despise—everything we feel we must reject in order to move into our individual selves. Our mothers represent oppression, failed dreams, disappointments. *My life will not be like my mother's.* This is the mantra of countless generations of daughters. I will not make my mother's relationship, career, or parenting choices. Her life will never happen to me.

Upon the shoulders of the mother rests the weight of the world. She is destined to fail her children, just as her mother before her failed her, and her mother's mother before her. Yet it is precisely these failings that inch future generations forward. The mother must, I feel, become a disappointment to the daughter, so that the daughter can begin to see her as human—so that an authentic relationship can emerge from the unrealistic expectations of both people. There cannot be a relationship of depth until mothers and daughters can view one another as separate human beings.

Yet this separateness is undeniably connected to a deeper sense of humanity. All of us came to this world through the body of a woman. The archetypal "Mother" figure is alive and well, even though our culture has tried desperately to deny her. In a patriarchal culture, there are not many places a woman can go to have her story valued. In a patriarchal culture, daughters are more apt to regard the mother as "less than" because that is what her society tells her. The ideas, plans, businesses, pay scales, and religions of men are regarded as greater.

If a daughter is trying to *not* be her mother, the most logical choice is for her to assume a stronger identity with the masculine. It is a normal response to reject everything and start again. As we mature, we discover the value in what we have rejected and begin to piece together a paradigm that suits us, incorporating traits from the past as well as from our own experience.

STRUGGLING TOWARD INTEGRATION

A total rejection of the mother is a rejection of the self. We are both women. Our relationships to our fathers are intimately connected to our relationship with our mothers and our acceptance or rejection of our feminine selves. To cut our mother out of our life is to cut out part of our heart. I come from two motherless parents. My mother's mother was an alcoholic and my father's mother hid behind the all-encompassing power of the Southern matriarch. Neither of my parents was nurtured by females. I am a product of them. How can I not assume some of their baggage? How can I not assume some of their pain? It is impossible. For though separation is essential to achieve individuation, the mature self does not emerge until integration is achieved.

I have discussed integration quite a bit as it relates to grief work. We must integrate the pieces of our story so we can build a whole. The same is true, I think, of the mother/daughter relationship. The struggle to maintain a complete separateness from our mothers leaves us scrambling, as daughters, to find our way. As we come closer to connection with our mothers and the archetypal Mother, we come closer to a path of wholeness.

While it is impossible to look at our stories and the things that have shaped us without looking at our family of origin, and our mother, especially, we will serve no one by assigning blame and calling upon a list of sins of commission and omission from our family. *Because we are not separate from one another,* it is impossible to assign blame to one person for acts done or undone without considering the context of that person's story.

When we, as daughters, are able to shift away from the belief that we are the center of our mother's universe, we will be able to see her story with greater compassion and empathy. This does not abdicate personal responsibility. If your mother physically abused you, that is not okay. But blaming her does not help you in your journey toward wholeness. Our mothers were not put on this earth to serve our every need. They are not here to be everything to us. And they are the product of another mother's story. And another mother before that.

THE BLAME CHAIN

Blame is a very aggressive act. It also prevents us from looking at the machinations of our own minds. It places our attention outward rather than inward, the only place we can achieve real satisfaction. If I can place responsibility squarely on the shoulders of another—whether it is for the traffic jam that "made me" late to work or the mother whose behavior "made me" who I am—then I refrain from taking responsibility for my own actions and choices. I remain forever victimized and powerless to the actions of others. This is an unhealthy place to be for both parties.

If I blame my mother, who can blame her mother, who can blame her mother, and the blame chain goes back until the beginning of humankind, what good have I achieved and what truth have I uncovered about either my mother or myself? Yes, we must acknowledge the truth of our relationships as we see it. We must also acknowledge that there are many truths. Relationships are not either/or constructs. When we can hold and embrace the complexity and contradictions of ourselves, we can hold and embrace the complexity and contradictions of others.

Looking at the mother/daughter relationship in the context of a grieving family is no easy task. If we are children or adolescents when we lose our dads, we emotionally return to a younger place when that loss occurs. We need our mothers in a way we may not have needed them the day before. Yet we also likely don't have tools for working with our feelings, so we don't know how to express those feelings to her. And our mothers are working with a profound loss for which they likely don't have tools. The resulting miscommunication and lack of communication can profoundly affect our attitudes and beliefs about the safety of the world.

Everyone's relationship with their mother, just like everyone's relationship with their father, is unique. My sister's relationship with our mother is not the same as mine. Sometimes, even in conversation, she will refer to Mom as "my mother" when talking to me, as if this woman were not my mother as well. This is not an attempt to diminish my relationship with Mom, it is simply my sister's unconscious awareness that her mother is uniquely "hers," whereas my mother is uniquely mine, no matter that we are talking about the same person.

How then, can our mother, a single human being with her own personal baggage, hope to be good enough and perfect enough for two separate and individual daughters? She cannot.

We've learned how the absence of the father causes disruption in the family dynamic. We've seen how it's impossible to maintain a family after the loss in the same way it was maintained prior to the loss. A family will change whenever change affects one of its members. Children are left to adapt to the new arrangement, often with little or no influence on it. Mothers are thrown into unfamiliar and unexpected roles at the time when their grief is at its worst.

Many mothers may be lacking the necessary education or skills to find a job that maintains the standard of living the family is accustomed to. Indeed, a lower economic standard of living is the norm for families whose fathers are absent. Children in these homes often experience a double loss—the loss of the father in addition to the loss of the mother from the home due to changed employment conditions.[1]

THE FATHER DEFICIT

There has been very little research done on the effects of working widows on their children. A widow is experiencing a great many things when her partner dies. She is "making internal and external changes to accommodate to changes in life circumstances, relationships, and sense of self."[2] She must go through her own meaning-making journey of the events that have occurred. And she must find a way to provide for her children. The ways in which she attempts to make meaning will depend on her age, her socio-economic status, her education level, her spiritual belief systems, and the amount of community support she has.

"My family was never the same after my father died," says Isabel, a forty-four-year-old registered nurse.

Janet's father died when she was fifteen. "Ever since my father died, my mom has been a little more on edge. My home life has really changed because my dad used to do everything around the house and now me and my mom have to, and it's hard."

In my case, my father dealt with the cars. When he died, my mother didn't know what to do with them. He cut the grass when he could. Even though he was very sick the last year of his life, he was still a presence in the house. Once he was gone, we became acutely aware of what he had done to help the household. I was already out of the house when he died. I remember my mother being slower with decisions. I remember her going to the grocery store on Friday nights after work because she couldn't bear to go home for the weekend.

My sister, who was still living at home, would remember different things if she were to speak about them. She was around Mom every day. I was in college. I remember feeling like I had no home anymore. I wanted to be seven years old, but I couldn't be.

My first apartment was not a home. Getting a place of my own had been exciting six months previously. Now it was a place to go and be alone. It was a place to reject everything our family had been struggling with during the last years of Dad's life. It was forced individuation. I had left the house and did not know how to go back, so I went further away from my mother and my sister. Dad's illness had been the focal point of the family. Once he was gone, I didn't know what kept us together.

Of course, I could not articulate these feelings at nineteen. I threw myself into school and work. I was determined to make a life for myself and not be torn apart by an event that we all knew was going to occur. But I just delayed my own grieving process. I finished school and I got a respectable job, but not until a decade after Dad's death, when I clearly saw myself trapped in a life I did not want, did I feel ready to do my own grief work and look at what was underneath our family mantra of "everything is fine." Looking at what emotions were locked under "everything is fine," embracing them, and releasing them, was my ultimate freedom.

In 2001 I began looking at my mother's relationship with her mother. I had put it off. When it would surface in a therapy session, I would gloss over it. I love my mother. I see the story of her mother etched firmly in her psyche. I see her coping mechanisms patterned after years of living with an alcoholic parent. I see her as a young girl, wanting her mother to embrace her but never receiving that touch. It is that young girl who I see when I want to know more about her life, or when I want to talk about Dad, or when I get angry.

I broke a Wiffle bat in an anger workshop when I was thirty-one. I responded, physically, to the chants of a dozen women saying, "everything is fine," banging drums, dancing, shouting. I kicked forward with a rage I had never before felt safe enough to express. I pounded a newspaper and pillow figure to death with my Wiffle bat, destroying the bat, losing my hair clips, and feeling, for the first time, how much energy I had been restraining.

In that workshop, I was finally able to say what I cannot say to my mother, and I was able to begin the process of releasing it. It is not my mother's fault that I was so angry. But nonetheless, I was so angry. Before I acknowledged that anger, it ate me, bit by bit. Once I acknowledged it, it no longer was necessary to confront my mother, either head-on or passive-aggressively.

I had let my own little girl loose, let her rage and stomp her feet, let her get exhausted so she could let go. It was a very powerful lesson in the energy of anger. When it is allowed to move through you, it purifies. When it gets stuck, it is toxic.

DAUGHTER SEE, DAUGHTER DO

Children will pay attention to what a parent does far more than what a parent says. A child picks up a mother's unspoken fears through her behavior, even if her language tells a different story. A mother who tells a daughter to go out and date and find companionship yet who herself remains at home and alone for the rest of her life is sending mixed messages. The child will absorb the message that is based in action.

If the mother is quick to remarry or find a new male partner to provide for her, the child may learn that a woman cannot survive on her own. We never know what pieces we integrate from our life experiences into our life's story. As children, our perception of a behavior may become translated into a belief system, even if that is in no way what the mother intended.

Taking on the role of both mother and father can be very taxing. It is not in the nature of the child to be aware of that. The child wants her mother unconditionally and with the same depth of presence as was there previously. The child wants to be heard, whether it's at three in the morning or in the middle of the workday. The mother needs to be able to find a support system for herself or she runs the very real danger of being wiped out by the demands on her.

It was not your job at thirteen to become your mother's support system. It was not your job to be her confidante or her confessor. But now, as adults, if you are carrying resentment toward your mother, you may have become aware of the fact that it only hurts you. It's true, in some circumstances, that it is best for you to not have your biological mother in your life. But for the vast majority of us, navigating the turbulent waters of the mother/daughter relationship is a lifelong journey. Undertaking the journey with an open heart brings us closer to one another and to ourselves.

Our mothers, like ourselves and our fathers, are not and never were perfect. Our fathers, however, have the opportunity to be perceived as perfect, now that they are gone. The mother is left to deal with the mundane, less than glamorous parts of existence. The father remains forever untainted by these things. If only Dad were here, he would have let me wear that dress, go out with that boy, stay out past midnight. And there is no way to prove otherwise because, of course, he is gone. So the mother is left to bear the brunt of our grief, dissatisfaction, and general adolescent angst. She may be vilified for even being alive. It is not unusual to wish she had been the one to die, not because we wish her dead, but because we wish our fathers back.

MOTHERS WHO DATE

A new man in the house is a challenge for the children, no matter the circumstances. Your relationship with your father and the circumstances surrounding his absence from the family will factor into how you adjust to your mother reconnecting with a man. Just like the way in which you were told about your father's death or leaving, the way in which you are told about your mother's dating has a significant effect on how you adjust to it.

Sometimes our mothers date a series of men, bringing more men in and out of the house than we would like. Sometimes our mothers never date again. Sometimes they date but don't bring their dates home. It is difficult to think of our mothers not just as human beings but also as sexual women with needs of their own. It is almost impossible, I think, for a child to understand the complexities of an adult intimate relationship.

The child has lost a father who can never be replaced. The mother has lost a companion, a mate, and a friend. But just as we have gone through our share of lovers as adults so can our mothers. A new lover does not diminish her feelings for your father. She is simply doing what is necessary for her to integrate and move fully into her life.

Problems arise when we try to judge our emotions with our intellect. Of course I intellectually know it is healthy for my mother to be in a new relationship. Of course I intellectually do not want her to spend the rest of her life alone. But I *feel* differently. Grief is a heart activity, not a head activity. Feelings don't make sense. Feelings don't need to be justified or rationalized. They just need to be acknowledged and they need to be felt. Then there's room for new feelings. Feelings that are not acknowledged or felt become lodged in our bodies, waiting for a moment to spring out unaware at someone else or ourselves. Feelings expressed in a healthy way cannot hurt us or anyone else. Their energy is transformed into healing.

You will never have another father. But you can have a relationship with the man your mother chooses. He will offer you different things than your father offered. You may wonder how your mother could have been with two such different people. You don't have to love him, but you could. You don't have to call him Dad, but you could. He is not your father, but he could still play a positive role in your life. The choice is yours.

Your mother is entitled to her life. She is entitled to her mistakes and shortcomings, just as you are. Her life, like yours, has taken unexpected turns. She is not all-powerful. She is a mirror for you just as you are a mirror for her. When you can put the mirrors down and look in each other's eyes, both your little girls will smile.

Writing Your Storyline

1. In general, how would you describe your relationship with your mother?

2. Tell the story of a time when you felt loved by your mother.

3. Tell the story of a time when you felt betrayed by your mother.

4. How would your mother describe you?

5. What are things your mother did not do for you that you think she should have done? Next to each answer, write down why you think she should have done it.

6. What do you want to tell your mother that you would never dream of telling her in person? Write a letter to her in which you tell her everything you've not been able to tell. Do not send the letter. If you are working with a therapist, you might read the letter to him or her.

7. If you could have the "perfect" mother, what would she be like? Describe her character, her dreams, her problems. How many of those qualities are present in your "real" mother? Tell the story of a time your mother embodied one of those qualities.

8. Assume you could step into your mother's shoes. What would her story be? Try writing a monologue from her point of view. You could focus on the day she found out her husband died, or found out she was being divorced, or the day she had to tell you what was going on, or the day she had to start working. Be as honest as you can be. Try to imagine what it was like for her. Remember our key writing points: be specific, use details. You might start with the line "I can't believe . . ." or "I don't know how to tell you . . ." if you need a prompt. When you finish this

exercise, write another letter to your mother. Write anything that comes up for you. Again, do not send the letter.

9. Did your mother remarry? If so, how did you find out about it? Tell that story.

10. If your mother is remarried, what is your stepfather like? Do you have contact with him? In what ways is he like your dad? In what ways is he different?

11. What would you like to tell your stepfather that you would never tell him? Write him a letter. Do not send it. If you are working with a therapist, you might read it out loud to him or her.

12. How does your mother speak about your father, if she speaks of him at all?

13. How did your mother change after your father's death or absence? This could involve physical changes, emotional changes, or spiritual changes. Be specific. How did you feel about these changes? Perhaps you were frightened. Perhaps you were lonely. Whatever you felt is perfect. Take the time to equate your feelings with the stories about the changes.

14. Ultimately, we are responsible for our adult lives. Inside each of us is a little girl. She is the part of us who dreams, who hopes, who believes in magic and possibility. She is the part who is wounded. You can take steps to re-parent and nurture her needs. Take this time to begin a dialogue with your inner child. Who is she now? What has happened to her? What does she want? What does she need? How can she integrate into your life? Let her draw a picture for you.

15. Write a letter as your adult self to your inner child. Allow her to write back to you. This meeting may take several weeks or longer. Many of us have hidden her and her needs away. She may be angry. Our inner child is emotional. She is not rational, not logical. Let her express her feelings without judgment from

your adult self. You might want to plan a date with her. Maybe she wants to swing, or go dancing, or fingerpaint. It is okay to play. It is okay to love yourself. Your inner child holds the grief of your father's absence. How has she held it? What can she tell you about it? You are the mother now. Listen with compassion and open your arms to her.

CHAPTER NINE

Complicated Mourning

JUST WHAT IS THE GRIEVING PROCESS? How do you know when you've done it? Do you ever finish? Can you do it wrong? Most of us don't spend any time on death education until someone we love dies. It is then, at the time of crisis, when we realize we have no idea what we're doing. We don't know what to do for ourselves, and we don't know what to do for anyone else. As adolescents, when we experience the death of someone close to us, our faith in the security of our own lives may be shattered. We are still in the throes of our "immortality" phase. We can't imagine ourselves one day dying.

If an adolescent girl experiences the death of her father, it is likely this is the first death of great significance that has touched her. What tools does she have to deal with it? We saw in chapter 5 how important the role of the family is in healthy grief processing. As an adolescent, you observed the coping skills that were being modeled to you by your family and friends. You looked to your community. If they did not have healthy tools, you would not have been able to get healthy tools for yourself. Since we may have "looked like" an adult, especially if we were in our late teens, we may have been overlooked while our mother focused on younger siblings. Maybe our mother simply wasn't capable of tending to our needs.

It is amazing to me that Americans know so little about the one event that is going to touch us all. I would like to introduce some terms. These came from Therese Rando's excellent book *The Treatment of Complicated Mourning*.[1] In it she tells us there are two general categories of loss. One is a physical loss, which is the loss of something tangible. Examples of a physical loss are the death of a loved one or pet, moving to a new house, or having your car stolen.

The second general category of loss is called psychosocial loss. Psychosocial losses are losses of intangible things, such as loss of hope or dignity, loss of a marriage, a child leaving home for college, or loss of mobility. All change involves loss. We often don't think of psychosocial losses as needing to be grieved, but they do.

ALL CHANGE INVOLVES LOSS

We must let go of something for something new to move in. Moving to California for your dream job may be a fantastic opportunity, but it means you will have to leave your home of twenty-five years in Boston. You may know the move is the right thing for you, but you still must grieve the loss of the life you built in Boston. When you don't allow yourself to experience the feelings that come from this change, those feelings will find a way to stay "stuck" in your body and psyche. Stories and rituals can help us grieve these normal life passages.

A secondary loss is a loss that "coincides with or develops as a consequence of the initial loss."[2] The death of a father creates many secondary losses. Not only have you lost your father's physical presence but you may have lost the financial security that his job provided. You may have lost your mother to her own grief.

You will also lose *any future relationship* with your father. For example, he will never walk you down the aisle at your wedding. He won't attend your college graduation. He won't hold your child. These are all secondary losses, which must also be mourned when they occur in much the same way that the primary loss is mourned.

Losing your dad in childhood means you were robbed of many defining moments that most girls with living fathers take for granted. We may have lost some of our childhood as we had to adjust our role in the family. Maybe we became the caretaker of younger siblings because Mom went to work. Maybe we gave up a chance to go away to college because we felt our family needed us. All these choices create a loss.

The grief process does not end. It is not linear. We don't proceed through a series of steps to achieve a prize at the end of the day. I think of the grief process as a spiral staircase going down. Down doesn't mean getting worse, it just means going deeper as we uncover the layers of things that have intertwined over the years. Each time you descend a floor, you get closer to the central issue, the root of your storyline.

The older we are, the more opportunity we have had to bury things in our psyches. We can create a well-fortified psyche with belief systems and storylines that no longer serve us. The grief work is our journey of discovery into the mysteries of our psyches. Sometimes we spiral in circles for a while. Sometimes we return with fresh eyes to the places we've already been. Each time we circle, we gain insight and wisdom. We are never done.

This doesn't mean when we experience a death that we can never live a happy and fulfilling life. It doesn't mean we don't know joy. I believe we can know an even greater joy, because it is the joy that comes from the awareness that there is suffering in the world. This joy comes from a new appreciation of each moment that was given to you. To live is to know loss. If we have the tools to move through the process of grief, we will gather many riches along the way.

THE ACTIVE WORK OF GRIEF

Grief work requires action. Sitting around and waiting for an appropriate amount of time to pass does not constitute grief work. Grief work means making active choices and changes that help to integrate the loss. Remember Worden's fourth task: to emotionally relocate the deceased and move on with life. This is integration. This is the re-storying.

Rando says that grief is actually the beginning part of mourning.[3] Grief is the response—the reaction. Mourning is the process of steps, stages, phases—whatever terminology you prefer. Mourning involves the things we do to help integrate the loss. In literature, the impact of grief on a story would be called the "inciting incident." It's the event that triggers the rest of the story. Mourning is the work—the physical, social, behavioral, and psychological steps we move through to gain integration of this loss into our story.

Sometimes we find ourselves stuck. Rando defines complicated mourning as a condition in which the griever either compromises, distorts, or fails to complete one or more of the normal mourning processes.[4] The reasons for the occurrence of complicated mourning are as varied as the individual. Remember that grief is an individual journey.

A person may not ever have the complete story about how the deceased's death occurred. This could cause complications in accepting the reality of the loss. Our attempts to make meaning from chaos begin the moment we find out about the death. We attempt to re-story our lives in such a way as to make the loss make sense. Unfortunately, what can happen is that we re-story in an unhealthy way or in a way based on incomplete information. If our foundation of basic pieces of information is not correct, what kind of narrative can we hope to form?

Sometimes we don't want to experience the pain. It can feel overwhelming and too much to bear. If we allow ourselves to feel it, it becomes real. We may not be prepared for that. Worden's second task (to work through to the pain of grief) may be compromised at this point. As adolescents, we did not have enough life experience to understand that we will live through this experience. We likely did not have a frame of reference. We may have been barraged with secondary losses that were beyond our scope to deal with. We may have had increased responsibilities that diverted our attention away from our grief work. We may have chosen to numb ourselves to the pain using any one or a combination of addictions. Anything we do that prevents us from fully feeling the loss prevents us from moving through our mourning work.

YOUR WORLDVIEW

We may be unwilling to let go of our assumptive worldview, that is, our belief system about how the world works. If we cannot create a story that integrates and incorporates the loss, we are unwilling to let go of our assumptive worldview. We are unwilling to let go of the way we think things should be. We are not able to let anything new in if we don't rewrite our old worldview. Sometimes that is too painful. We cannot imagine a life without the deceased, so we refuse to have one. We sabotage our own happiness and our own lives. We can't go back in time and change the past, but we can change the way we relate to the past. This is the power of story.

I did not know anything about the concept of unresolved grief or complicated mourning when my father died. I had known since I was seven and he became ill that I had been living with the story of his impending death. I didn't know until much later how much that storyline became interwoven into how I viewed the world. When he died, I identified with the loss. I shaped my identity around the loss. This wasn't conscious; it was simply all I knew to do.

I had begun creating a storyline for all future relationships around loss and abandonment. I succeeded in manifesting that storyline with every relationship I encountered. It is true that we cannot go back and change the past. But we can change what we choose to take with us from the past, and we can change the way we relate to the past.

UNRESOLVED GRIEF

I experienced unresolved grief after my dad died. Unresolved grief is connected to incomplete relationships. This means, essentially, that when a relationship ends we are not through with what we needed or wanted from that relationship. We still have unfinished business. When someone close to us dies, we very likely have unfinished business with them. We wish we could say something, or take something back, or experience something one more time. This is normal.

We get stuck when we can't integrate the loss. We are incapable of writing a story that does not include the deceased *as we knew him*. Sometimes we can even develop an intimate relationship with that pain and loss. We can become addicted to our feelings of loss or sadness. This sets up a powerful cycle of relationship with pain. The question surfaces: who would I be if I let my sadness (or rage) go? We have become so enmeshed in a belief system and storyline of anger, betrayal, and abandonment that we fear if we let it go we will have nothing left. We all need storylines to function in the world. We have control over whether or not those storylines are in our best interests. When we release, we can re-story. Then we become the authors of our own lives.

Here are some warning signs of unresolved grief:

- severe depression
- hypochondriasis
- psycho-physiologic reactions
- alcoholism
- drug dependency
- psychotic states
- inhibited or absent grieving[5]

Substance abuse occurs frequently in an attempt to avoid feelings about the loss.[6] When a person is not able to feel the normal feelings of grief associated with the loss, she is not able to move through the grief process. When a person dies, it is *normal* to cry, or to rage, or to express your unhappiness in other ways that are nonharmful to yourself or others. In our society today, we have a tendency to medicate whenever we feel the least bit of discomfort. If the feelings don't surface, they get stuck. Worden's second task (to work through to the pain of grief) is critical. We have to feel it to move through it. The good news is it's never too late to go back and re-experience the pain. We must *fully feel the loss* so we can re-story our lives in an integrative way.

Mourning is not considered complicated until the symptoms persist for more than a month following the loss. We are *supposed to feel* a wide range of conflicting emotions immediately following the death. A person unable to function three days after the death is normal. A person unable to function three months after the death should seek help. No matter how much we may rely on our intellect in our daily lives, our intellect cannot move us through grief.

Worden's fourth task (to emotionally relocate the deceased and move on with life) is easier said than done. To clearly move into this space, we must be able to fully release the idea that our relationship with our father will never be the same as it was when he was alive. We must be able to release the idea that he is coming back or that he will do or not do something for us. For some time, we may intellectually know that he is dead. But the heart quite often takes a much longer time to catch up.

The phone rings and you think for a split second it could be him. You think you catch a glimpse of him in a car next to you, or in an elevator just before the doors close. These are very common experiences for grievers. The heart has not recognized the permanence of the loss. The brain is sending out projections, hoping for a connection with the lost "object" (father). The heart is clinging to any hope at all that the loss did not occur.

NO QUICK FIXES

As with all grief work, there are no hard and fast rules. Grief is an individual process. Because there is such an absence of healthy dialogue about grief in our culture, people look for the quick fix for grief. There is none. When determining whether or not you have unresolved grief, look at your ability to function *completely* in the present world. Examine your ability to trust others. Notice if you are a whole part of your world. Many of us are forced back to work days after the loss occurred. Just because we can go to work and earn a paycheck doesn't mean we are functioning completely and wholly in our world. Look at your heart. How open is it?

Quite often, our real feelings and motives are hidden in our unconscious minds. We would never say, "Oh yes, I am choosing to spend my life alone and without love and support because I know that no one will ever love me as much as my dad." But perhaps that is the belief system that is running our lives. We may not say, "I will not date anyone because I know that all men leave. If my dad left me, then I am clearly unlovable. All men are destined to leave me." Yet that might be what our unconscious mind is working with as we navigate our life.

Therapy can be very valuable for uncovering hidden belief systems. It is difficult to do this work alone. I mentioned in chapter 1 that I was surprised to find I had hidden belief systems around becoming a writer. Once I brought those belief systems to my conscious mind, I was able to rewrite them in a way that better served me. I had a pattern in intimate relationships of choosing men who were clearly emotionally or physically unavailable. I continued to ignore the obvious signs that they would not be able to give me what I needed, and I was continually surprised when they did not meet my needs. My storyline, unconscious though it was, did not serve me. But until I became aware of it, I was unable to change it.

Many women bring their deceased father into their current intimate relationships. Some of us do it consciously, some of us unconsciously. I became so afraid of being left again that I internalized my dad as a "guard" to protect the castle of my heart. He would not let in anyone who could hurt me. But of course, he turned away everyone, because there is always a chance for hurt when we take a chance to love. I didn't realize this. Instead of serving as a healthy advisor in my relationships, he took them over. But I could not have told you that. Through therapy I became aware of it and was able to "emotionally relocate" him to a place of service for me rather than destruction.

As I said, there are no rules for what is a healthy or unhealthy relationship with your dad. For some people, keeping a shrine of photographs or mementos helps keep him close by in a healthy way. For others, keeping a shrine may indicate an unwillingness to move through to the pain of grief. The absence of photographs or mementos is also a revealing detail. However, before an assessment can be made, one must look at the individual, her particular psychology, her culture, and her life before the deceased passed away. Self-awareness is key. What is okay for you may not be okay for your sibling or your mother. This is one of the trickiest parts of grief. We have to allow our loved ones to work through their grief in their own ways.

You know in your heart whether or not you are holding on too tightly. I used one of the exercises in this chapter to write a poem about what I felt I was still carrying.

Burdens

I gathered rocks today.
One for each of you.
I tried to choose the size, the texture, the color
that best suited you and me
and the story I have written.
I wrapped them all, six of them,
with crimson twine,
bound them to another rock,
and I carried them
today,
physical, heavy, jagged.

I carried them up hills
into bedrooms and into kitchens.
It didn't take long (a minute or two)
to realize they were too heavy
to keep carrying like this.
I would have to devise another method
if I were to keep it up.

I was angry to have them.
Angry to keep them,
and each time I picked them up they got heavier
until I finally laid them down
and when I closed the door
I didn't miss them
and I could still see the sun.

If you think that you are holding on too tightly, just for today, write down in your journal, "I release you, Dad." Just for today. Breathe. It took many years to establish your belief systems. They will not be undone in five minutes. When you are able to think about him, talk about him freely, and remember the gifts he gave to you without a debilitating longing for more, you are integrating. There will always be moments of sadness around his death, especially at special occasions where his absence is most noticeable. Sometimes a song or a scent will still make you cry. That's normal.

To move through to the pain of grief doesn't mean you don't still miss him. It means you no longer cling to an unattainable hope that you will have him with you again in the same way. Or, if he was abusive or emotionally unavailable to you, you are no longer clinging to the unattainable hope that he will have been any different during your childhood.

A place of calm acceptance emerges. For me, I quite literally saw colors differently after I integrated Dad's loss. They were more vibrant. I saw possibility instead of disappointment. I took healthy risks that a year before would have been unthinkable. I could feel my body taking up space in the world in a more complete way. My posture improved. My eating habits improved. Not through conscious efforts to change them. They were a natural result of release. Yours will take the form that is necessary for your growth. Just know that letting go of the attachment to your dad does not mean you lose him. In fact, he becomes available to you in a way that was never possible when you held onto the hope of having him back as you knew him.

Even if you have been stuck in grief for many years, you have still gained great insights during those years. Honor your experience, whatever it has been.

Writing Your Storyline

1. What do you miss the most about your father?

2. What physical items, if any, do you have that were his? Where are they in your home?

3. Where do you keep pictures of your dad? How many are visible and where are they?

4. What did your dad say to you that you still remember? These can be positive or negative things.

5. Intuitively, how do you feel you carry your father's memory with you? Where is it in your body? What does it look like? How much does it weigh?

6. How often do you talk about your dad to family or friends? When you do, what feelings, physically and emotionally, surface for you?

7. What are the emotional triggers for you around your father's memory? For example, are you unable to have a banana split at Baskin Robbins because you and he used to go there after your softball games? Or do you feel the tears come when you smell a certain aftershave? What things elicit memories from you about him? Be as specific as you can. What do you do when the feelings surface?

8. Have you used avoidance tactics, such as alcohol or other drugs, to avoid the pain? If so, what and for how long?

9. If the information in this chapter felt familiar to you, are you willing to examine your belief systems on a deeper level? If not, that's okay. You may be ready at another time. If you're ready now, try this:

- Finish this sentence: "When Dad died, I . . ." Freewrite for fifteen minutes.

- Finish this sentence: "I am most afraid of . . ." Freewrite for fifteen minutes.

- Finish this sentence: "If I changed the way I currently live, I would . . ." Freewrite for fifteen minutes.

- Finish this sentence: "If I let go of my attachment to Dad, I would . . ." Freewrite for fifteen minutes.

- Finish this sentence: "Because Dad isn't here, I can't . . ." Freewrite for fifteen minutes.

- Finish this sentence: "Because Dad isn't here, I can . . ." Freewrite for fifteen minutes.

- Finish this sentence: "I'm not happy with my life right now because . . ." Freewrite for fifteen minutes.

- Finish this sentence: "If only Dad had . . ." Freewrite for fifteen minutes.

- Finish this sentence: "If only Dad hadn't . . ." Freewrite for fifteen minutes.

Take your answers to your counselor, therapist, or support system. Talk through your process with someone who is a detached, caring companion on this journey with you.

10. You have decided that it is time to let things go. You've done the remembering and the reconnecting exercises. You're ready to experiment with a new story. Here are some suggestions:

- Gather rocks, each rock representing something you are carrying that you don't want to carry anymore. You can name or label your rocks. Put them in your backpack or purse and carry them around for one day. At the end of the day, decide which rocks you want to get rid of and remove them from the bag. Carry the bag with you the next day. Journal about the difference in weight.

- Stand, feet parallel, big toes touching each other if possible. Inhale deeply, raising your arms overhead. Exhale, audibly, as you fold forward, letting your head and your hands hang toward the ground. It's okay if you can't touch the floor. Just allow yourself to hang, head heavy, arms heavy. Take three deep inhales and exhales. Slowly return to standing. Take one more full breath in and out. Go to your journal and write whatever comes up.

- Write a letter to your dad. Tell him everything you want to say. Don't censor yourself. It's okay if you're angry. It's okay if you cry. Just write until there's nothing left to say today. Do this every day for a week. At the end of the week, you may burn or bury the letters.

- Take a look at how you completed the sentences in exercise 9 of this chapter. Mark sentences and paragraphs where you would like a new story. Pick one that feels particularly important to you today and rewrite (re-vision) the work. Be specific. Release all limitations. Don't worry about whether or not you "believe" you can have or do or be the things you're writing about. Just write. Remember to breathe. When you're finished, read your new story out loud to yourself.

- Draw a picture or make a collage that represents what you would like to bring into your life. Use images and words.

CHAPTER TEN

Intimacy:

Looking for Dad in a Mate

Permanence

I am too much alone and never alone enough.
I curse the ringing of the phone and then wail in its silence.
I pray on my knees for human touch then push it away when it arrives
silent and swift in darkness.
I remain as I have always been—
Convinced of the permanence of that illusion.
    —LH

"Whether I stay with you or not, I will not bring your father back."
My lover, exasperated, said this to me as we were separating. "No
matter what I do, he won't come back."

I was so angry I had to go outside. I was surprised by our
breakup. I had believed he wanted to commit to me. He had just
driven to Los Angeles for my graduation and had been talking
about moving in with me. This was not the conversation I expected
to have. Yet as I stood outside, the spray from the fish pond cool on

my skin, I knew there was truth in what he said, although I had no idea how to articulate it. I wanted to scream at him, hit him, break his glasses across his nose, and crush his guitar to splinters, but even as I wanted to do these things, I was unsure who in me was doing that wanting.

I didn't really want to hurt him. I loved him. Yet his desire to end our intimate relationship unleashed a rage I did not know was there. This man was the first man who I felt loved me as I was. He honored my writing. He honored my spirit. He helped and encouraged my growth. He reminded me, in so many ways, of my father.

I'd like to say I was Buddha-like and went back inside and had an enlightened conversation with him about all my unconscious desires, but that was not the case. Instead, I went back inside and began a series of "shadow attacks" on him that came from, I thought, nowhere. We spent the next three years navigating my grief work, although he had taken a new lover. I began to see exactly where those "shadow attacks" were coming from, and I may well have been the only one surprised.

He left me, but he stayed. His ability to stay with me, to love me and grow with me while I worked through these new awarenesses, helped me write a new storyline about men and about love. I didn't *have to be abandoned* anymore. I did not have to continue to seek out men who could not commit to me so I could reenact the abandonment storyline. My father wasn't coming back. He had been dead fourteen years at the time of this encounter, but I *just then*, at the moment my lover spoke those words to me, knew it was true.

You may recall this is Worden's first task: to accept the reality of the loss. It was necessary that this man end our relationship so that the awareness of the unconscious pattern could surface. His ability to articulate what I was really raging against and to hold the space around it helped me, over time, to feel safe again. Learning to trust in a man's love was another important part of rewriting the storyline. He never did "leave" me, and slowly I began to awaken to the possibility of a different story.

MEN WHO LEAVE

Once I became aware of the pattern, it was crystal clear what was going on. I was choosing men who told me, repeatedly, that they could only stay a little while, and then I was surprised when they indeed could only stay a little while. It was as if I thought each time, "Well, this one is different. He'll see how wonderful I am and he won't leave me." But each time, each man did leave. This reinforced the abandonment story. It never occurred to me that *it was possible* for me to make different choices. I was so firmly entrenched in my belief that any man who loved me deeply would abandon me that I could not allow for the possibility that one might stay someday.

I didn't know what my unconscious was up to. I learned that often people will unconsciously choose patterns to repeat that still need healing. I learned that unfinished business and incomplete relationships don't go away on their own. I knew I needed to really examine my storylines and see how and where they connected to Dad's death if I ever hoped to have a successful partnership with a man.

The quest to understand what belief systems I had internalized was the birth of this book. I wanted to find out what was *really* governing my choices so that I could make different choices. I wondered if other women who lost their fathers during adolescence experienced similar problems with intimate partnerships. The research and their stories helped me feel less alone. It normalized my behavior, which also helped provide a safe place to do the revisioning work I needed to do in order to move fully into my life.

In the introduction of this book, my poem "Trapped" illustrates this feeling of being entwined with the memory of my father in a way that was detrimental to a healthy life. Here is the last stanza.

> *I will have died with you,*
> *your skeleton locked around me.*
> *If only you would move your arm I could stretch,*
> *but you can't because you're dead*
> *and I, dutiful daughter,*
> *will never break that bone.*

When I wrote the poem, I did not consciously know what I was writing about. It was an interesting image to me, but only in retrospect did I see how much my unconscious was trying to tell me. My own creative work continues to show me things I am not consciously aware of. I have learned to trust in the process of the work and release the outcome. I encourage you to do the same.

UNRAVELING THE BALL OF YARN

Everything is connected. The stories of our lives take twists and turns when events happen and we, as the main character in our lives, respond in ways that are familiar. We respond with the tools we have. We take into consideration the responses of those around us. As children, we are seeking storylines to help us deal with the problems of our lives. We absorb the dynamics of our family. We then have our own belief system created from all the places we can get input: our culture, our social groups, our family, our faith. This is why two people growing up in the same household can take two very different approaches when death comes to the house. We all have our own individual mythology, our own personal story about how the world works and how we fit into it.

If, as an adult, you have experienced difficulty relating to and maintaining intimate relationships, it is worth examining the effects of your relationship with your father on your storyline. But it is important to remember that it is enmeshed with your other personal beliefs, so it is part of a greater "whole system" of beliefs.

Think of your belief systems as a big ball of yarn. Each belief system has its own color, so everyone's ball of yarn is a mass of colors, but it's a single piece of yarn. One color bleeds into the next, so when we examine and rewrite one belief system, it affects the system's whole. When we change one area of our lives, we also change other areas. We can't help it—they are all connected.

The way your father died, or the way your father maintained or did not maintain a relationship with you after a divorce, or any number of things, can contribute to a belief system, but none is the only factor to consider. This is helpful when we do our work because it shifts the focus away from blame. Blame doesn't serve anyone, most especially you.

It can be very helpful, however, to become aware of common characteristics we have with other women who experienced similar things. This is very normalizing, and can be quite a relief when you see you're not the only one to have felt or done certain things. When I began talking to other women about their stories, I felt very validated, and understanding that other women had made choices similar to mine or had complications similar to mine made it easier for me to look at my own belief systems. Prior to that, before the sharing of stories, there had just been silence. When we can share our stories, we open our hearts. Sometimes our storyline itself can be so contained in darkness and secrecy that the act of bringing it to light shifts it.

CONNECTING WITH MEN

Researchers have identified some common characteristics for girls whose fathers died. Claudette Grimm-Wassil concluded that females whose fathers died tended to have the most positive concept of their father while feeling the most sad about his disappearance. They also tended to avoid contact with males.[1] In terms of sexuality, daughters of widows were likely to be scared of men.[2]

Earlier in this book, we discussed the possible qualities of daughters whose parents divorced. These qualities included intensified separation anxiety, denial and avoidance of feelings associated with the loss of the father, identification with the lost object, and object hunger for males.[3]

For most of us, our father was the first man in our lives. From him we learned how to interact with other men. Our relationship with our father teaches us how to connect with the "other." Our relationship with our mother shows us what is acceptable for our own gender; our relationship with our father shows us what is acceptable for us in our relationships with men.

THE EGO

The ego often gets a bad rap in our culture. The ego is the container for your growth and your life. Healthy ego development occurs in childhood. Having a healthy ego does not mean you are conceited or narcissistic. It means you have a solid foundation for who you are and how you operate in the world. Healthy ego development is essential for creating and navigating a healthy life. A strong ego provides healthy boundaries for you to grow and evolve. A strong ego provides a solid container for you to completely feel your emotions. You can fall into your sadness without fear it will swallow you whole. You can participate in relationships as an autonomous being rather than enmeshing yourself in the lives of others. You are, truly, the heroine of your own life.

Many of our adult problems can be traced to an incomplete ego development. We did not gain a solid sense of self as a child. We did not grow up feeling the world was safe and therefore we cannot take risks. We did not have a harbor to return to, so we felt uneasy about exploration. The ego is instrumental in our personal growth work. It holds us while we fight the dragons. It is our *known* conscious operating system for our world. Jung's work introduced the idea of an equally powerful unconscious mind that he believed was truly guiding our lives. Bringing the unconscious belief systems into the realm of the conscious mind is a process of integration. It is the cornerstone for a new storyline.

A WORD ABOUT PATRIARCHY

Feminism can be a much-maligned term. Women who call themselves *feminists* can be labeled any number of negative adjectives. I include this section because I believe that to understand how, as young women, we learn to relate to men, we cannot dismiss our culture. Patriarchy, as it has evolved, harms both women and men. Patriarchy is a social system in which men are the authority within the family and the society. Men, in many respects, still hold the power cards. The last fifty years have seen some great strides in women's rights, but we are still far from an equitable society.

The older I get without marrying, the more of a societal oddity I become, no matter what my other accomplishments may be. I feel that in American society women are still invisible without the approval stamp of a man. It's no wonder that women seek relationships with others before a relationship with self. It's no wonder that when our relationships don't work out, we may feel that we have no worth or value. When who we are and what we bring to the table is not valued, then most of us look to be enmeshed in the world of one who does matter—one who is seen—and for many of us, that is in relationships with men.

A woman growing up in a patriarchy knows, without ever having to be told, that she is not as good or as valuable as the men in her society. Countless studies have documented how girls defer to boys in school during adolescence. It's not desirable to be smarter than the men, so we tailor our lives around pleasing our men.

What does this have to do with grieving our fathers? I think quite a bit. In a society where men are more valued than women, gaining the love, affection, and attention of our fathers is of primary importance to girls. We need to be seen by men in order to have any power in this culture. If we are not seen by our fathers while growing up, what choices are left for us in adulthood? If we are rejected by the first man in our lives, where can we possibly find a place to belong in a culture that values men more?

Most people today will not say outright, "As a culture, we value men more than women." It's much more subtle, and I think far more dangerous, because lip service is paid to a different belief system that is not manifested in the culture. Yes, there have been great changes, but they have been primarily surface changes. Evolution takes a long time. We have not yet begun to cellularly change the belief system of American patriarchy. Look at how your father was treated within your family. This shaped your belief system around men. How did your father respond to his role? How did he treat the rest of the family? How did he treat you compared to your brothers? How did he treat your mother? All these factors contribute to how you developed as a young woman.

Was your father "king of his castle" or was there a partnership within the family? Did your mother adjust her life to meet his needs or did your mother and father have healthy lives, separate from one another? Did your mother have outside friends and activities that did not involve your father, or was that "not allowed"? When your father died, or left, how did your mother respond? Did she "replace" him right away? Did she curl up and retreat from life? Or was she able to move forward in spite of the radical changes in her world?

Children learn much more by observing than by direct information. You were affected by the dynamics of your parents' relationship. Much as your relationship with your father was your first relationship with a man, the modeling your parents did for you of a marriage formed your first, foundational belief system around what partnership looks like. It is important to know what you've internalized and what you believe about men in general before examining how current intimacy patterns may be affected by your relationship with your father.

FIRST LOVE?

Women are trying to connect with their inner masculine, just as men are trying to connect with their inner feminine. We, as developing girls, are not hungering for our father's penis in a romantic or sexual way. We are naturally curious about the "other," but children do not understand Eros yet. The seven-year-old girl is not developmentally capable of consciously seducing her father. Yet she may very likely adore him. She may place a greater value on what he has to say than what her mother says. She may want to marry someone "just like Daddy." This is not because she is in love with her father.

Robert Johnson discusses the concept of being "in love" as a shadow projection of what is divine onto another human being. Our unrecognized or unacknowledged divinity gets projected outward, dooming both parties to disappointment and dissatisfaction. Being "in love," he proposes, will transform into love based in reality of the other's faults and your faults. Being "in love" cannot last because it is rooted in illusion; love, however, is eternal.[4]

Are we "in love" with our dads? For most of us, the answer is no. Do we tend to long for someone who embodies the traits that we found most appealing in our dads? Very likely, yes. However, if our dads did not provide us with safety and a solid foundation, we may still find ourselves drawn to men who show us those qualities—not because we consciously desire to be hurt again, but because we are drawn toward what is familiar.

Many of us read books or watch films over and over again. This is not because we are so stupid we didn't get it the first time. It's because we are comfortable with the familiarity of the stories and the characters. The surprise ending from the first time is nowhere near as surprising the tenth time we see the film. Abandonment storylines may hurt us each time the ending comes around, but there is a part of us, relaxing in our unconscious, saying "Oh yes, I know this part. I've been here before," and that part takes comfort in this illusion of control. When the same story plays itself out over and over again, the security net of our belief system is maintained. We are in no danger of change or growth and we sink into the pain of familiar patterns. The status quo wins again.

It takes a great deal of courage to break an abandonment storyline. The possibility of a different outcome can be extremely frightening. Yet it is only through rewriting our storylines that we can hope for a different outcome.

DATING, VIRGINITY, AND DADDY

"Daddy's little girl" will, at some point, be involved with another man. She will start to date. She will experiment with her sexuality. She may get married. Her father, who was once her shining knight, will be replaced by a pubescent boy with acne and braces. He will be replaced by a man dressed in black leather with a tattoo on his neck. He will be replaced by the bookworm from her AP physics class. It doesn't matter whom he is replaced by—there will be many throughout the daughter's life.

What does matter is how both father and daughter adapt to these fundamental passages in each other's lives. The relationship is changing for both father and daughter. The father, as the adult, has the responsibility for setting and maintaining healthy boundaries and ensuring that his daughter is allowed to become a woman, separate from him. This can be very challenging for many fathers.

A father has enjoyed his daughter's admiration and doesn't want to share it with another male, especially one he doesn't feel is worthy of his daughter. The daughter, completely immersed in teenage hormones, may abandon her father for boys her own age. This is not an intentional attack; it is a normal growth process for her. She must separate from her father so that she can interact in a healthy way with other men. Knowing her father's love is constant can be a great source of comfort for her on this exploration.

Unfortunately, this is not always the case. This normal adolescent passage from the home nest can be severely compromised when the girl's father is dying or leaving the home. It is the *father's role*, not the daughter's role, to stand back and let her take her first steps into adulthood. It is his role to be there when her heart gets broken, and it is his job to be there when she is ready to fully separate by leaving the house. When he is not there, she is left to her own devices to navigate the realm of men. When he is not there, there is no male to reinforce safety and stability.

When we begin to date, our tendency will be to behave with the boys we date in the same ways we behaved with our fathers. This is, after all, how we learned to interact with men. If we were silent until our father spoke, we will likely abdicate our power in our dating relationships. If we agreed with whatever our father said because it maintained the peace, we will likely continue this pattern. If we learned to flirt and manipulate to get our father's attention, we will likely do the same with the boys we date.

DATING AND SEXUAL ENCOUNTERS

Dating has changed drastically in the past fifty years. The girls of my mother's generation did not interact much with boys until they began dating. Dating was more formal, perhaps more awkward. In my generation, I don't recall many people actually "dating." People hung out together, went to the mall or to a movie, slept together, broke up, moved along in relatively short time frames. Most everyone I knew by the time I was sixteen had been sexually active.

Today, with the prevalence of HIV and other sexually transmitted diseases, dating has shifted again. Though there is a large celibacy movement for teens, most teens have experimented with sexuality. Oral sex has become the replacement for intercourse for teens afraid of pregnancy. The prevalence of sexual imagery and sexual information today has demystified much of the sexual experience.

The ways boys and girls interact with each other today is much more informal and comfortable. I see boys and girls in the schools I work in behaving in a much more natural way with one another than even my generation. I think this is ultimately a good thing. If the opposite sex is not so much a mystery, we are more comfortable being ourselves. If boys grow up knowing girls have brains, talents, athletic abilities, and dreams of their own, they will, I think, be less likely to expect all that to disappear once they become intimate partners with women.

Virginity is a much talked-about issue today. I think there is still a prevalent belief system around the virgin/whore paradox for women that does not exist for men. A woman who is free and confident in her sexuality still risks being labeled a whore. The derogatory terms for sex with women and women's body parts lay the foundation for detachment during sex, rather than connection. If a woman is her parts, then anything can be done to her. If a woman is a whole being, it is more difficult to cut her or rape her or molest her.

One of the challenges of the adolescent passage is sexuality. The body is ready and capable of sexual activity and reproduction. There are huge outside pressures to become sexually active. But we are still girls, and the people we have sex with are still boys. I don't know that we can fully understand the value of sex until we have experimented with it. I don't see how we can know what we give to the men we sleep with until we know what we lose when we give it to the wrong men. I think it's important to think about how you lost your virginity in the context of the father/daughter relationship.

I also want to examine the language of the phrase "losing our virginity," as if we dropped it somewhere in the parking lot. Language, as we've learned, is very powerful and can create many unhealthy belief systems. If I "lose" my virginity, that implies no conscious intention to share my sexuality with another person. Does the man "find" it? Where, exactly, does it go?

For many of us, our first sexual encounter may have been awkward and unsatisfying. Neither person knows what to do or has any framework for the potential of what it can be. Often there is relief after the first time. If we still lived at home, coming back to the family after having sex for the first time shifts things in the family dynamic, whether we talk about it or not. And it is highly unlikely that we talked about it.

YOUR REAL SELF

We cannot be truly intimate with another person until we have learned to be intimate with ourselves. I'm not talking about masturbation, though that is certainly a healthy component of self-care. I am talking about a healthy, complete relationship with your Self. This takes time. A seventeen-year-old is not developmentally capable of knowing who she is and what she wants. She is exploring, and that is exactly what she should be doing. But as we age, our relationship with our Self grows. We begin to see that we will not be "completed" by another person.

The right man will not make our lives okay. If we are constantly seeking relationships to avoid solitude, we will not find what we are looking for. Partnership can enhance a life, but ultimately, you are your own friend, lover, and companion. When you are able to commit to your Self, you are able to then commit to another.

Many women get swept up in the Prince Charming myth. If we expect our partners to make everything right within our Selves, we set ourselves up for disappointment. No one can do that for you, just as you cannot do that for your partner. Two autonomous, growing, aware people can walk a path together that enhances both journeys. But when one partner expects the other to fill the emptiness in his or her own soul, the pair is headed for trouble.

As we learned, the defining question of adolescence is "Who am I?" When we date and experience sexuality as adolescents, we are still grappling with that question. We have a different perceived identity when we date the football captain than when we date the chess team champion. We have a different perceived identity when we are sexually active compared to girls who are not sexually active. "Who am I?" and "How do I fit into this world?" are not questions we escape in our sexual lives.

You may know adult women who cannot seem to function without a man. They move from relationship to relationship, searching for the "one" who will rescue them from themselves. But they won't find him. The answer is within. How do you feel when you are involved with a man? How do you feel about yourself when you are not? What do you believe a man brings to a relationship with you? What are your expectations of that relationship? What do you believe being in a relationship will provide you? Are they realistic expectations?

These are belief systems to examine when you choose intimate partners. Relationships help us grow. We need people in our lives. They help us uncover unconscious patterns and can provide a safe space to work through our baggage. Everyone comes to the table with baggage. No one is perfect and no one will meet your every need. The doors to intimacy open when we acknowledge fully what we have to offer and what we still carry with us.

If we have not completed our relationship with our fathers, whether he is living or dead, we may choose men to partner with who will help us complete that relationship. Completion simply means finishing what is still unfinished. As in my example, I chose men who were not available to me in an unconscious desire to fully experience the loss of my dad. My unconscious knew where I was stuck, even though I did not. It knew that I had to acknowledge the reality and the finality of that loss before I could find true intimacy.

Some of the exercises at the end of this chapter will help show you patterns you may be experiencing. These are guideposts for you on your journey. Only when patterns are revealed and acknowledged can they be changed. Each awareness is a gift. Treat it as such and don't judge yourself.

I believe that one of the most fascinating things about stories is that when conflicting storylines occur, one storyline has to dissolve. You can only live so long in a world that does not fit with your storyline. If one of your storylines is that you are beautiful and deserve to be loved and to give love, you will not be able to operate very long in a story where you are abused. It just doesn't fit.

Conversely, if you believe you don't deserve to be loved, you will have a challenging time fitting into a story where you are loved. Remember that many of our belief systems are unconscious. You may say, "Of course I deserve to be loved," but you may unconsciously believe exactly the opposite. What story do you want to participate in? Only the characters that will fit in that story will appear for you. The same characters don't appear in a mystery novel as appear in a horror novel as appear in a literary novel. They wouldn't fit. Examine who and what fits into your story. What storylines do you fit into? What ones do you not fit into? Are you living in ones where you don't fit?

An excerpt from a poem I wrote when I was struggling with understanding who I could be if I were not sad all the time reads, "If I send Sorrow away/and there is room on the bed/what would happen?" New characters could come in. New stories. Imagine that.

Writing Your Storyline

Again, these exercises are not designed to be worked through in fifteen minutes. They are designed to help you discover more about yourself and your stories so you can better prepare for your journey toward intimacy. Work with a therapist whenever possible. Be honest, be specific, and be nonjudgmental.

1. Brainstorm around the word "men." Whatever comes up is perfect. Try setting an oven timer for fifteen minutes and write.

2. Finish this sentence: "Compared to women, men are . . ." Freewrite for fifteen minutes.

3. Finish this sentence: "If I were a man, I would be able to . . ." Freewrite for fifteen minutes.

4. Finish this sentence: "Because I am a woman, I am unable to . . ." Freewrite for fifteen minutes.

5. Make a chart of qualities of both genders. Put male qualities on one side and female qualities on the other side. There is no right and wrong to this.

   • Circle the qualities from either gender that you feel are qualities your father possessed.

   • Tell a story about a time you used one or more of the qualities you listed on the male side of the chart. What occurred? Who was involved in the story? What was the outcome? How did you feel about yourself?

   • Do the men you date embody any of the circled qualities?

6. Describe your dad's personality. What did you like the best about him? What did you like the least about him?

7. Finish this sentence: "I loved it when Dad would . . ." Freewrite for fifteen minutes.

8. Finish this sentence: "I always hoped Dad would . . ." Freewrite for fifteen minutes.

9. Examine your last three intimate relationships with men. Take each relationship separately. If you are in a marriage or long-term partnership, still take it back three times. First describe the

man. Then write the story of the relationship. How did you meet? What did you do together? What did you talk about? What were your expectations for the relationship? What were his? What events led up to the breakup of the relationship? Be honest. What did you learn from each encounter?

10. Create a chart or graph of intimate relationships. Include every man you have been sexually intimate with to the best of your knowledge. If you can't remember a name, just write an "X" but still include the encounter. You might start with your most recent or current relationship and work backward. You might start with the first man you were sexual with. It doesn't matter. Everyone has her own sexual history. Be honest. Don't judge how many or how few encounters you have had. It doesn't matter. What you're doing is looking at your stories. Underneath or beside each encounter, write down characteristics or traits of that person and that relationship. What did you like best about him and that relationship? What did you like least? When you are finished, look for similarities and differences among the men and the experiences. How, if at all, do they connect to the qualities and desires you had for your relationship with your father? Don't force an answer.

11. Tell the story of your first sexual intercourse experience. Remember to include the moments leading up to the encounter and the moments after the encounter. Don't just include the series of events. Include your feelings and recollections about the events. What expectations did you have? Did you want to do it? What led up to your decision to have sex that moment with that person? A word of warning: If your first sexual experience was forced, write that story as well. If your first sexual encounter was incestuous, write that story. If either of these last two fit your storyline, I encourage you to speak to a counselor who can help you work with the issues that surface from sexual abuse. It is beyond the scope of this book to ad-

dress it, but it is crucial you tell your story and begin to work with how it shaped you.

12. Finish this sentence: "When I am in a relationship with a man, I . . ." Freewrite for fifteen minutes.

13. Finish this sentence: "When I am not in a relationship with a man, I . . ." Freewrite for fifteen minutes.

14. Finish this sentence: "If I were to be open and intimate with a man, I would . . ." Freewrite for fifteen minutes.

15. Finish this sentence: "I am afraid that if I found a partner, I would . . ." Freewrite for fifteen minutes.

16. Finish this sentence: "I am afraid that if I left my partner, I would . . ." Freewrite for fifteen minutes.

17. Finish this sentence: "I believe in order to be in a relationship with a man, I will have to give up . . ." Freewrite for fifteen minutes.

18. Finish this sentence: "A man in relationship with me needs to give me . . ." Freewrite for fifteen minutes.

19. What is different about your life when you are in an intimate relationship? Think about your career, your family, and your friends. How do these other relationships shift? What is the same about your life when you are in an intimate relationship?

20. If you are not currently in a relationship, do you want to be? Why or why not? If you do, write a story of what that relationship would look like. Remember to include the moments leading up to it and the moments after you are fully in relationship.

21. What do you bring to your intimate relationships? These can include positive and negative qualities.

22. Being in intimate partnerships requires risk. We have to believe the risk is worth the reward. All relationships bring us growth

and awareness. Finish this sentence: "To risk is to . . ." Freewrite for fifteen minutes.

23. Draw a picture of you and your partner. If you do not currently have a partner, draw a picture with you and another person. You can leave the face blank or fill in the facial features. What internal qualities and traits do you want this next partner to have? You can write the words on your drawing. If you are currently with a partner, write down the internal qualities and traits you see in him. Again, notice how this may or may not compare to the qualities you expressed about your father. Notice how it may or may not compare to the qualities of other partners you have had.

24. Finish this sentence: "A healthy partnership for me looks like . . ." Freewrite for fifteen minutes.

CHAPTER ELEVEN

Release, Renew, Rebirth

One day I opened the window
and Grace splashed in, dripping,
shaking her wet head and smiling.
"I thought you'd never let me in," she said.
"Me neither," I said, "but I am so glad."

I wrote this poem in 2002. I had completed a very intense therapy cycle and I was letting go of many unconscious patterns. I was beginning, for the first time in my adult life, to allow for the possibility of joy and community.

The work is never done. We move through cycles, always aware that each uncovering, each understanding, is the gateway to newer, deeper understanding. Life is a process of continued growth and change. We only have to look to nature to see this process is a part of all life. Times of dormancy are normal. Times of death and decay are normal. Times of joy, life, and vibrant color are normal. All of it is impermanent, and rather than mourning the fact that it is impermanent, look at the truth. All life is impermanent. Then choose what story you want to tell yourself about that truth.

Our suffering does not come from the truth. It comes from the story we tell ourselves about that truth. Yes, when someone we love dies or leaves, we mourn that loss. But we can become addicted to the mourning just as we can become addicted to alcohol or gambling. And when we become addicted to the mourning and the sorrow, there can be no room for other stories. Our unique story has the ability to open us up to the wonder of life. Our stories heal us, hold us, nurture us. Our stories show us the way home.

Your father was a real, flesh-and-blood human being with whom you were in a relationship. That relationship changed. You were left to create a new story without him. We were often not ready to do this. We still wanted our daddies. We still wanted life to go on as it was before. We can invest a great deal of energy into that wanting. That wanting will never be satisfied, and we will continue to be unhappy, longing for things to be different. I am not trying to take away the normal sadness, anger, or melancholy that surfaces when someone dies. We must *feel all our feelings*. Denying them causes damage. But just as we cannot hold onto a kiss, we cannot hold onto our grief if we hope to live fully.

This may sound simplistic. It is both the most difficult and most simple thing you will ever do. I can think of nothing else that so fully embraces the paradox of life. I took a seminar many years ago that dealt with resentments and anger. The presenter asked for volunteers. Three people were called up to the front of the room. The person in the middle was carrying anger and bitterness. The people on either side of her represented her anger and bitterness. The presenter instructed the woman in the middle to grab onto the wrists of each of the people. She did. Time passed. We all wondered what this was about. The woman in the middle kept holding on. The two people on her sides did nothing; they just stood there. About five minutes passed before the presenter asked us what was happening. We didn't know. He asked us to look at the three people more closely. Who was holding on? Who had the power to let go? What were anger and bitterness doing to keep her there? Absolutely nothing. It was a powerful demonstration of how we carry our emotions with us, and how unattached our emotions are to whether they are there with us or not.

Sometimes we have held on so long we cannot imagine what it would be like to let go. Who would we be? If I let my sorrow go, who would be left? Do I have any tools to navigate a world in which that storyline is not dominant? This can be a very frightening place to be. It is the middle passage—the dark road through the forest where we have no guarantees what is waiting for us on the other side. We only know that we can no longer stay where we have been. This takes a tremendous leap of faith.

I was in a yoga class where the practice was to pause between postures to integrate the movement of energy. It's a tempting time to adjust your strap, wiggle your fingers, or play with your hair. I was doing that when the teacher walked by and whispered, "What if you didn't fidget." The fidgeting was such an ingrained reaction to stillness that I had never considered the possibility of a reality that did not involve fidgeting. He planted the seeds for a new storyline in five words.

Change doesn't happen overnight, but it can happen deeply when we begin to re-story. Even though I may still fidget from time to time, I hear my teacher's voice and I am able to examine the reality, *for just that moment,* of not fidgeting. Then I am able to observe what a life without fidgeting would look like. Try this work on a day-by-day basis. What if, just for today, you did something loving for yourself? What if, just for today, you entertained the idea of a different life? You can always return to the life you know if you want to.

LETTING NEW THINGS FIND A WAY IN

Just for today, let in a new paradigm. You could start with something as simple as a new color in your wardrobe or a new pair of glasses or shoes. How would life be different if you wore jeans today instead of a tailored skirt? How would life be different in thong sandals compared to three-inch pumps? What if you painted your toenails red instead of your usual beige? Just a little bit at a time. There's no need right now to gut your house and buy a new wardrobe and get different friends. It takes time to decide what you want to release and what you want to continue to carry forward with you.

Sometimes we have to purge a lot. Sometimes we just have to re-align things. If you purge everything too quickly, you may find you've let go of something or someone who is still valuable to your life. If you haven't purged your life in some time, you may be over-whelmed by the task. Take a little bit at a time. When you let go, there is room for things you have not anticipated. When you hold on, the new things cannot find a way in.

Letting go of your father does not mean you forget about him. It doesn't diminish in any way the depth of the relationship you had with him. I remember in the months after Dad's death, if a day passed when I didn't think of him, I would cry and feel horrible. I didn't think it was okay to not think about him every spare mo-ment I had. I didn't want him to feel lonely, and I thought if no one thought of him, he would then, truly, be dead.

But the truth was that he was dead no matter whether I thought of him or not. I remember the first year the anniversary of his death passed without my awareness. I certainly had not forgot-ten he was dead, nor had I forgotten he had been alive. Researcher Craig J. Vickio writes that when we are aware of the unbroken con-nection between the living and the dead, we can gain a sense of im-mortality.[1] I feel that our awareness of these connections also provides a powerful foundation for the next chapter of our lives. It is a great relief to not have to cut out of our memory a person whom we have loved. It is a great relief to know he can still walk our life path with us.

Time shifts our stories. The process of life involves continuously adapting to change. When a death occurs, the adaptation to this new story is time-consuming. It wasn't part of the plan. We rebel against it. We rage. We negotiate, bargain, and attempt to make it something different than what it is. Eventually, unless we wish to continue living our lives in the tableau of the past, we must make a new story.

How? Every daughter must find her own path. For me, the re-storying took a decade. Each relationship brought a greater awareness. Each problem, each challenge, showed me something new. For me, the day arrived when it was no longer okay for life to continue as it had been. I had known, intellectually, that I was stuck for many years. I was stuck in a city I did not like. I was stuck in a story of loss and sadness that continued to repeat itself. I embraced my solitude like a lover. And one day it hit me: What if I didn't fidget? What if I didn't believe I had to be alone? What if I didn't believe I could only find work in Phoenix, Arizona? What if? And then, for me, I knew I had to do what I had never done. I had to move out of my father's house.

He had died before I could consciously separate. His death had brought me back to him in a way neither of us could have anticipated. His death had solidified my eternal childhood. I saw that I could not fully move into my own house (life), as long as I was still living in his. And I saw that I, like the woman I described in the demonstration, was the one holding onto him. He was not attached to me.

What did this mean? It meant that I had to say good-bye and mean it. I had to tell him I was moving out. I had to claim my life. I went to the cemetery to tell him. I brought a significant object from my childhood. I sat there, all the while thinking, *It's not too late. You can still go home. You don't have to do this now.* So I sat longer until my mind had run its course. I sat until the sun set and the Arizona air cooled. I put the object on the gravestone. I told him I was moving to Prescott. I told him I couldn't come home anymore, that I was ready to live in a world without his physical presence. I told him I had a room for him at my new house, but he could no longer have the whole house.

I wanted what was best from him, what he had taught me, what he had given me. I wanted to take those things and build a future with them. I told him it was okay that he died, and that his death had given me my life. I cried a lot. And then I stopped. And I stood up, blew him a kiss, and drove away. I put my house on the market and moved to Prescott, Arizona. To others, it seemed like a quick decision. But I, and my father, knew it had taken seventeen years. My new story has the essence of him in it, just as it has the essence of everyone who has participated in my life. But it's now my story.

Worden's fourth task is to emotionally relocate the deceased and move on with life. I did not know what it meant to "emotionally relocate" someone. It sounded very "New Age." Here's what it means: Take the essence of your relationship with your dad and give it a place in your heart where it can nurture you. Give it a forwarding address that is close enough to visit, but not so close you can never bring in anyone new. Claim your whole life, including the influences of your father.

"Moving on" does not mean forgetting. It does not mean never crying again or never wishing he were still here. Moving on means walking into your life consciously, with the benefits and wisdom of all the experiences that brought you to this place. It means saying "yes" and honoring the totality of your experience. It means crying and laughing, risking and planning, trying and failing. It means living.

What does your true voice sound like? What does she want to say? What has she been holding back? It is a process to find our true selves. We will experience many false starts and failures. But each experience brings us closer. Each connection shows us a different way of speaking and of being in the world. When our authentic voice is narrating our story, the world opens. What story do you want to write?

Born Again

I went to the closet to put on my past
as I do every morning about this time.
When I buttoned the starched, blue cotton dress shirt
my breasts spilled through the buttonholes like syrup.

When I stepped into my black leather boots
the heel broke off and I walked, lopsided, through my day.

The elastic on the flowing cotton skirt was stiff and dry and the skirt fell around
*　　my ankles in a puddle of neon tie-dye color.*

One by one the buttons popped off the blouse
leaving me exposed and breathing,
naked, fresh, waiting to be written upon.

Today I stood before the open window
sticky from birthing fluids
on my head
between my legs
underneath my feet.

My past in mothball-eaten ribbons
unable anymore to hold me in
disintegrates like scorched elastic
leaving a trail of cotton dancing on the closet floor.

This is what it means
to be born again.

I stand in circles of tears I have owned
and I have swum through,
my mask gray with fog
from breathing underwater.

This is what it means.
New eyes.
New mouth.

My lungs blow letters.
Letters hold hands and wrap around and underneath
my tongue until I cannot help but
shout.

This is what it means
to breathe.

Writing Your Storyline

1. Examine your current relationship with your father. Remember that even if he is dead, you are still involved in a relationship with him. How high a priority is your relationship with him? You might try answering this question: how often do you think about your dad? The goal is not to dissolve your relationship with your father. The goal is to re-create a relationship that is healthy for you.

2. Finish this sentence: "I think about Dad the most when . . ." Freewrite for fifteen minutes.

3. Finish this sentence: "My father's memory feels like . . ." Consider giving the feeling a weight or a color or a texture. Freewrite for fifteen minutes.

4. Finish this sentence: "If I let you go, I'll . . ." Freewrite for fifteen minutes.

5. Finish this sentence: "If Dad were here today, he'd . . ." Freewrite for fifteen minutes.

6. Draw a picture of your heart. Fill in with color the place where your dad lives. Notice how much is filled. Does it feel healthy to you? Fill in with other colors other people whom you love. Examine the relationships among the colors. What do you notice?

7. Finish this sentence: "Starting today, I will . . ." Freewrite for fifteen minutes.

8. How is your life different without your father? Can you identify any positive differences? What skills did you learn as a result of his absence or death?

9. Write a letter to your father thanking him for the gifts he has given you. Be specific about what they are. Tell him what is going on in your life. Tell him about your dreams and plans. Wish him well, if you choose. Read it out loud. You might like to burn or bury the letter when you're finished.

10. Create your own ritual to honor your past relationship with your father and usher in a new relationship with him. Some things you might like to use are objects from your past, a special song or poem, or a phrase that only the two of you knew. It doesn't have to be elaborate. It's your relationship, your ritual, your release. Write down your feelings before and after the ritual. Breathe.

11. Celebrate. Take a long walk or a bubble bath. You might like to get a manicure or a new haircut. You might like to play an instrument or watch a favorite movie. Do something that is just for you that makes you feel good. Welcome yourself into the next phase of your story. Welcome home.

Notes

Chapter One: Grief Counseling

1. J. William Worden, *Grief Counseling and Grief Therapy: A Handbook for the Mental Health Practitioner*, 2nd ed. (New York: Springer Publishing, 1991). © Springer Publishing Company, New York 10012. Used by permission.

2. Therese A. Rando, *The Treatment of Complicated Mourning* (Champaign, Ill.: Research Press, 1993).

3. John W. James and Russell Friedman, *The Grief Recovery Handbook: The Action Program for Moving Beyond Death, Divorce, and Other Losses* (New York: HarperCollins, 1998), 3.

4. Marie Louise von Franz, "The Process of Individuation," in *Man and His Symbols,* ed. C. G. Jung (New York: Dell, 1964), 174.

5. C. G. Jung, *The Archetypes of the Collective Unconscious* (Princeton: Princeton University Press, 1990), 282.

6. Joseph Campbell, *The Hero with a Thousand Faces* (Princeton: Princeton University Press, 1973).

Chapter Two: What Is Adolescence?

1. Judith Herman, *Father-Daughter Incest* (Cambridge, Mass.: Harvard University Press, 1981) cited in Lyn Mikel Brown and Carol Gilligan, *Meeting at the Crossroads: Women's Psychology and Girls' Development* (Cambridge, Mass.: Harvard University Press, 1992).

2. Helene Deutsch, *The Psychology of Women* (New York: Grune and Stratten, 1944); Karen Horney, "The Flight from Womanhood," *International Journal of Psychoanalysis* 7 (1926): 324–39; Clara Thompson, *Interpersonal Psychoanalysis* (New York: Basic Books, 1964) cited in Lyn Mikel Brown and Carol Gilligan, *Meeting at the Crossroads: Women's Psychology and Girls' Development* (Cambridge, Mass.: Harvard University Press, 1992), 2.

3. Lyn Mikel Brown and Carol Gilligan, *Meeting at the Crossroads: Women's Psychology and Girls' Development* (Cambridge, Mass.: Harvard University Press, 1992), 5.

4. Erik H. Erikson, *Identity: Youth and Crisis* (New York: W.W. Norton, 1968).

5. Jung, *Archetypes of the Collective Unconscious,* 275 (see chap. 1, n. 5).

6. Charles A. Corr, "Entering into Adolescent Understandings of Death," in *Bereaved Children and Teens,* ed. Earl Grollman (Boston: Beacon Press, 1995), 24.

7. David E. Balk and Laura C. Vesta, "Psychological Development during Four Years of Bereavement: A Longitudinal Case Study," *Death Studies* 22, no. 1 (January/February 1998): 23.

8. James W. Pennebaker, *Opening Up: The Healing Power of Expressing Emotions* (New York: Guilford Press, 1997).

Chapter Three: The Father/Daughter Relationship

1. Alan L. Wineburgh, "Treatment of Children with Absent Fathers," *Child and Adolescent Social Work Journal* 17, no. 4 (August 2000): 255.

2. Victoria Secunda, *Women and Their Fathers: The Sexual and Romantic Impact of the First Man in Your Life* (New York: Delacorte, 1992), 27.

3. E. Mavis Hetherington, "Girls Without Fathers," *Psychology Today* (Feb 1973): 47–52.

4. Secunda, *Women and Their Fathers.*

5. Maureen Murdock, *The Hero's Daughter: Through Myth, Story and Jungian Psychology, An Exploration of the Shadow Side of Father Love* (New York: Fawcett Columbine, 1994).

Chapter Four: Fathers Who Died: Long-Term Illness, Accident, Sudden Death, Homicide, and Suicide

1. Tim O'Brien, *The Things They Carried* (New York: Penguin, 1990).

2. James and Friedman, *Grief Recovery Handbook,* 111 (see chap. 1, n. 3).

3. Ibid.

4. Kenneth J. Doka, "When Illness Is Prolonged: Implications for Grief," in *Living with Grief When Illness Is Prolonged,* ed. Kenneth J. Doka (Washington, D.C.: Hospice Foundation of America, 1997).

5. Therese A. Rando, ed., *Loss and Anticipatory Grief* (Lexington, Mass.: Lexington Books, 1986) cited in *Living with Grief When Illness Is Prolonged,* ed. Kenneth J. Doka (Washington, D.C.: Hospice Foundation of America, 1997), 35.

6. Ibid.

7. Kenneth J. Doka, "Sudden Loss: The Experience of Bereavement," in *Living with Grief after Sudden Loss: Suicide, Homicide, Accident, Heart Attack, Stroke,* ed. Kenneth J. Doka (Washington, D.C.: Hospice Foundation of America, 1997), 11.

8. Stephen P. Hersh, "After Heart Attack and Stroke," in *Living with Grief after Sudden Loss: Suicide, Homicide, Accident, Heart Attack, Stroke,* ed. Kenneth J. Doka (Washington, D.C.: Hospice Foundation of America, 1997), 17.

9. D. Lehman and C. Wortman, "Long-Term Effects of Losing a Spouse or Child in a Motor Vehicle Crash," *Journal of Personality and Social Psychology* 52, no. 1 (1987): 218, 231 in *Living with Grief after Sudden Loss: Suicide, Homicide, Accident, Heart Attack, Stroke,* ed. Kenneth J. Doka (Washington, D.C.: Hospice Foundation of America, 1997).

10. National Highway Traffic Safety Administration (NHTSA), Fatal Accident Reporting System (August 1995) in Janice Harris Lord, "America's Number One Killer: Vehicular Crashes," in *Living with Grief after Sudden Loss: Suicide, Homicide, Accident, Heart Attack, Stroke,* ed. Kenneth J. Doka (Washington, D.C.: Hospice Foundation of America, 1997), 25.

11. Janice Harris Lord, "America's Number One Killer: Vehicular Crashes," in *Living with Grief after Sudden Loss: Suicide, Homicide, Accident, Heart Attack, Stroke,* ed. Kenneth J. Doka (Washington, D.C.: Hospice Foundation of America, 1997), 26.

12. Ibid., 30.

13. www.ojp.usdoj.gov/bjs/homicide/homtrnd.htm

14. Ibid.

15. www.ojp.usdoj.gov/bjs/homicide/gender.htm

16. Deborah Spungen, *Homicide: The Hidden Victims, A Resource for Professionals* (Thousand Oaks, Calif.: Sage Publications, 1997), 23.

17. Lula M. Redmond, "Sudden Violent Death," in *Living with Grief after Sudden Loss: Suicide, Homicide, Accident, Heart Attack, Stroke,* ed. Kenneth J. Doka (Washington, D.C.: Hospice Foundation of America, 1997).

18. Ibid.

19. Mary S. Cerney and James R. Buskirk, "Anger: The Hidden Part of Grief," *Bulletin of the Menninger Clinic* 55, no. 2 (Spring 1991): 228.

20. Ibid.

21. Ibid.

22. Redmond, "Sudden Violent Death."

23. Ibid.

24. Spungen, *Homicide.*

25. Ibid.

26. J. L. McIntosh, "Control Group Studies of Suicide Survivors: A Review and Critique," *Suicide and Life-Threatening Behavior* 23, no. 2 (Summer 1993) in Judith M. Stillion, "Survivors of Suicide" in *Living with Grief after Sudden Loss: Suicide, Homicide, Accident, Heart*

Attack, Stroke, ed. Kenneth J. Doka (Washington, D.C.: Hospice Foundation of America, 1997), 42.

27. www.cdc.gov/ncipc/factsheets/suifacts.htm

28. Judith M. Stillion, "Survivors of Suicide," in *Living with Grief after Sudden Loss: Suicide, Homicide, Accident, Heart Attack, Stroke*, ed. Kenneth J. Doka (Washington, D.C.: Hospice Foundation of America, 1997), 42.

29. B. G. Allen, L. D. Calhoun, A. Cann, and R. G. Tedeschi, "The Effect of Cause of Death on Responses to the Bereaved: Suicide Compared to Accident and Natural Causes," *Omega* 28, no. 1 (1993–1994): 39–48 in Judith M. Stillion, "Survivors of Suicide," in *Living with Grief after Sudden Loss: Suicide, Homicide, Accident, Heart Attack, Stroke*, ed. Kenneth J. Doka (Washington, D.C.: Hospice Foundation of America, 1997).

30. Stillion, "Survivors of Suicide," 50.

Chapter Five: Fathers Who Were Absent: Divorce, Abandonment, Incarceration, and Addiction

1. Franklin B. Krohn, "The Effects Absent Fathers Have on Female Development and College Attendance," *College Student Journal* 35, no. 4 (December 2001): 598.

2. www.divorcenter.org/faqs/stats.htm

3. Claudette Grimm-Wassil, *Where's Daddy? How Divorced, Single and Widowed Mothers Can Provide What's Missing When Dad's Missing* (Woodstock, N.Y.: Overlook Press, 1994).

4. E. Mavis Hetherington, "Effects of Father Absence on Personality Development in Adolescent Daughters," *Developmental Psychology* 7 (1972): 313–26.

5. R. Lohr, C. Legg, A. Mendell, and B. Reimer, "Clinical Observations on Interferences of Early Father Absence in Achievement of Femininity," *Clinical Social Work Journal* 17, no. 3 (1989): 351–65.

6. Grimm-Wassil, *Where's Daddy?*

7. Krohn, "The Effects Absent Fathers Have," 598.

8. Cynthia Beatty Seymour, *Parents in Prison, Children in Crisis:*

An Issue Brief (Washington, D.C.: Child Welfare League of America Press, 1997), 3.

9. D. Gilliard and A. J. Beck, "Prison and Jail Inmates at Mid-year 1996," *Bureau of Justice Statistics Bulletin* (Washington, D.C.: U.S. Department of Justice, 1997) in Cynthia Beatty Seymour, *Parents in Prison, Children in Crisis: An Issue Brief* (Washington, D.C.: Child Welfare League of America Press, 1997).

10. Seymour, *Parents in Prison*, 7.

11. Seymour, *Parents in Prison*.

12. D. Johnston and M. Carlin, "Enduring Trauma Among Children of Criminal Offenders," *Progress: Family Systems Research and Therapy* 5 (1996): 9–36 in Lois E. Wright and Cynthia B. Seymour, *Working with Children and Families Separated by Incarceration: A Handbook for Child Welfare Agencies* (Washington, D.C.: Child Welfare League of America Press, 2000).

13. Lois E. Wright and Cynthia B. Seymour, *Working with Children and Families Separated by Incarceration: A Handbook for Child Welfare Agencies* (Washington, D.C.: Child Welfare League of America Press, 2000), 24–25.

14. Claudia Black, *Straight Talk from Claudia Black* (Center City, Minn.: Hazelden, 2003).

15. Ibid.

16. Stephanie Brown, "Addiction as a Family Disease," in Drew Pinsky et al., *When Painkillers Become Dangerous* (Center City, Minn.: Hazelden, 2004).

Chapter Six: Broken Passage: Incomplete Adolescence

1. Erikson, *Identity* (see chap. 2, n. 4).

2. Ibid.

3. Diane Zimberoff and David Hartman, "The Ego in Heart-Centered Therapies: Ego Strengthening and Ego Surrender," *Journal of Heart-Centered Therapies* 3, no. 2 (Autumn 2000): 3.

4. Ibid.

5. D. K. Lapsley, K. G. Rice, and G. E. Shadid, "Psychological

Separation and Adjustment to College," *Journal of Counseling Psychology* 36 (1989): 286–94.

6. Reprinted with permission of Simon & Schuster Adult Publishing Group from *A Music I No Longer Heard: The Early Death of a Parent* by Leslie Simon and Jan Johnson Drantell. Copyright © 1998 by Leslie Simon and Jan Johnson Drantell, 36.

7. Ibid., 139.

Chapter Seven: Family Dynamics

1. Ellen F. Wachtel and Paul L. Wachtel, *Family Dynamics in Individual Psychotherapy: A Guide to Clinical Strategies* (New York: Guilford Press, 1986), 5.

2. Brown, "Addiction as a Family Disease" (see chap. 5, n. 16).

3. Ibid., 154.

4. J. William Worden, *Grief Counseling and Grief Therapy: A Handbook for the Mental Health Practitioner*, 2nd ed. (New York: Springer Publishing, 1991). © Springer Publishing Company, New York 10012. Used by permission.

5. John P. Geyman, "Dying and Death of a Family Member," *The Journal of Family Practice* 17, no. 1 (1983).

6. Victoria H. Raveis, Karolynn Siegel, and Daniel Karus, "Children's Psychological Distress Following the Death of a Parent," *Journal of Youth and Adolescence* 28, no. 2 (April 1999).

7. Ibid.

8. Ibid.

9. Lauren Saler and Neil Skilnick, "Childhood Parental Death and Depression in Adulthood: Roles of Surviving Parent and Family Environment," *American Journal of Orthopsychiatry* 62, no. 4 (1992).

Chapter Eight: The Mother/Daughter Relationship

1. Elena Duckett and Maryse H. Richards, "Maternal Employment and the Quality of Daily Experience for Young Adolescents of Single Mothers," *Journal of Family Psychology* 9, no. 4 (1995): 418–32.

2. Marion M. Danforth and Conrad Glass Jr., "Listen to My Words, Give Meaning to My Sorrow: A Study in Cognitive Constructs in Middle-age Bereaved Widows," *Death Studies* 25, no. 4 (2001): 513–29.

Chapter Nine: Complicated Mourning

1. Rando, *Treatment of Complicated Mourning* (see chap. 1, n. 2).
2. Ibid., 20.
3. Ibid.
4. Ibid.
5. www.journeyofhearts.org/jofh/grief/warnings
6. www.medterms.com

Chapter Ten: Intimacy: Looking for Dad in a Mate

1. Grimm-Wassil, *Where's Daddy?* (see chap. 5, n. 3).
2. P. Adams, J. Milner, and N. Schrepf, *Fatherless Children,* (Ontario, Canada: John Wiley & Sons, 1984).
3. Grimm-Wassil, *Where's Daddy?* (see chap. 5, n. 3).
4. Robert Johnson, *Owning Your Own Shadow: Understanding the Dark Side of the Psyche* (San Francisco: HarperSanFrancisco, 1991).

Chapter Eleven: Release, Renew, Rebirth

1. Craig J. Vickio, "Together in Spirit: Keeping Our Relationships Alive When Loved Ones Die," *Death Studies* 23, no. 2 (March 1999): 161.

Index

About the Author

LARAINE HERRING is an author and teacher. She holds an MFA in creative writing and an MA in counseling psychology. She currently teaches at Phoenix Community College, Yavapai College, and Rio Salado College, and in the MFA program at Prescott College. She has developed numerous workshops that use writing as a tool for healing through grief and loss. She is also a novelist and editor, and her work has been widely anthologized. Her work has been nominated for a Pushcart Prize. She lives in Prescott, Arizona.